THE

KNOW-IT-ALL

GIRL

THE
KNOW-IT-ALL
GIRL

Joanna Foreman

A Memoir by a Former Jehovah's Witness

Hydra Publications | Madison, Indiana

Hydra Publications
337 Clifty Drive
Madison, IN 47250

Printed in the United States of America

www.hydrapublications.com

For Emma

FOREWORD

By Richard E. Kelly

After reading *The-Know-It-All-Girl*, I thought about the advice Socrates gave at his trial for heresy, "The unexamined life is not worth living." Definitely not something you could say about Joanna Foreman after reading her eye-opening memoir. The similarity is that Socrates spoke those words to encourage his students to challenge the accepted beliefs of the time and to think for themselves. Joanna *shows* that message in a well-written book that will make you laugh, cry and think.

Joanna is not a preacher or a Socrates-want-to-be philosopher. She is a gifted storyteller with a most unusual, comedic story to tell about a girl and a woman who must navigate through life in a high-control religious environment, in a *Cuckoo's Nest* world. If you've been there, done that, and you're a woman, you will be able to relate. If high-control religion the way Jehovah's Witnesses play the game is foreign to you, be prepared for an entertaining education.

This book is not a story of blame and resentment. Yes, there are the side-effects of forty-five years of cult life, but Joanna honors the positive aspects as well. It's the rich imagery of the characters that will dazzle you, like Joanna's imaginary friend Dainy, her best friend Emma and the fun-loving, sometimes ditzy Joanna waltzing her way through life.

When Joanna asked for my advice about this book, I encouraged her to tell it all. She needed to reveal the good, bad and the ugly. She far exceeded my expectations, leaving no stone unturned, and I believe you will find that to be one of the most endearing aspects of her story.

The-Know-It-All Girl could have been written only by a woman. It's the kind of book I wish my sister Marilyn would have had the opportunity to read before her untimely death. She, like Joanna and me, was raised as a Jehovah's Witness—a cult that treats women as second class citizens, claiming that women were created by God solely for the purpose of serving man as a helpmate. Reading Joanna's story would have been an inspirational experience for Marilyn, as I believe it will be for most women.

Richard E Kelly,
Author of *Growing Up in Mama's Club*

ACKNOWLEDGEMENTS

It took a village to get this book into your hands. Richard E. Kelly, author of *Growing Up In Mama's Club*, mentored and inspired me throughout the entire project. My youngest son, Jordan T. Coe, who attended the University of Iowa and majored in Creative Writing, used his editing skills to tighten my manuscript, and his numerous side notes with his recollection of certain events were, in the end, more accurate than my memories.

I've driven my family crazy by asking them to reminisce about our time in the Organization, but they graciously took those trips with me back to the past so I could make sense of what we'd all experienced together. Everything written is the truth as I recall it, and I believe my memories are reliable. Certain names and locations have been changed in order to protect the privacy of those concerned.

The Southern Indiana Writers' Group definitely deserves a shout out—in particular T. Lee Harris and Marian Allen, who insisted I put a certain novel on the shelf and write this memoir NOW. It's ill-advised to argue with higher intelligence.

Frank Hall at Hydra Publications merits my utmost gratitude for putting this book into print and online. T. Lee Harris for the cover art, and my editor, Martha Swanson, worked tirelessly and offered their professional ideas, which I gratefully accepted.

INTRODUCTION

While attending a week-long writing conference in Taos, my class of ten students and one instructor sat around a conference table with our assignment: *If I had one year to live and could be quite prolific I would . . .*

(I continued until the three-minute timer went off.)

" . . . write my memoir, not titled Running With Scissors, but Running With The Blinders Off, a story about how for forty-five years I was literally stuck (by choice) in a religion which discouraged college, did not allow thinking for oneself, holiday celebrations, voting, pledging of the flag, or standing for the National Anthem.

For over a decade, my life without blinders has been spent trying to catch up with the rest of the world. It's a spiritual life, but without the religion that interfered with my spirituality. I cast it aside. I now see the world in an entirely new light.

Sometimes it's blinding without the blinders on."

After I read this out loud, the students applauded and our instructor leaned toward me, aiming her pointer finger at my nose. *"That* is marketable!"

I'd considered writing this story specifically for my family but had never dreamed it might be of interest or value to others. During the next few days, several students approached during our breaks, persuading me to write a memoir. They asked questions about my former religion and suggested my viewpoint would be helpful to all sorts of people trapped in unhealthy situations.

So I decided to tell my story, hoping it would encourage readers to see their own light. I referred to old journals and diaries and developed friendships with other ex-Jehovah's Witnesses in Facebook Forums, people like me who were navigating a dark passageway through their past. During the writing process I learned something dreadful about myself, that for over four decades I'd actually believed I knew it all!

Writing has been a healing process twisting through the maze: anger, pain, hurt, frustration, and fear of leaving old friends behind—to reach my Paradise on Earth. And yes I found it, once I took my blinders off.

PART ONE

CHAPTER ONE
IMAGINARY FRIENDS

"Treat your child's imaginary friend with respect. This means remembering his name, greeting him when you meet, and apologizing when you sit on him." ~ Armin Brott

Other little girls on Stratford Avenue were lucky enough to have older siblings who spoke words of wisdom and served as tour guides through the perils of youth. But not me.

Grandma was my tour guide until I was five. Then she went away. That's when I discovered Dainy. She was the first to speak.

"Poof! Here I am," Dainy said, "three days after your grandmother went to heaven. Such an unusual state of affairs, I'd say. What's the meaning of this?"

"I'm lonely now. I have no one to play with."

"I get it . . . you invented me. So . . . am I supposed to be your grandmother reincarnated or what?"

"No, silly girl. I don't believe in that." I paused for a moment. I didn't even know for sure what the word *reincarnated* meant. "Umm . . . well, actually I don't know *what* I believe. Anyway," I said as I waved her off the subject, "I'm much too young to think about it."

Obviously, Dainy had snooped inside my closet to retrieve a dog costume. She'd forced the Lone Ranger-style mask up underneath the white hood, on top of her very straight bangs, causing her black dog ears to stand upright. "Just so you know, I'm not the fairy godmother type," she said. "I'm your *imaginary* friend, okay?" She pulled white paw covers over her hands and struck a dance pose, paws on her hips.

I had to admit she was rather cute, but I hadn't expected her to be in the middle of an identity crisis at such a young age. "I know *exactly* what you are," I said, heaving a lengthy sigh so she'd see how exasperating she was.

"Good! And while we're at it, here's a word of advice. Since you have no specific beliefs yet, don't go around asking questions. They'll put you in the box labeled Religion with a capital R. Mark my words."

I shrugged, not because I didn't care about what she'd said, but because I didn't want *her* to know I cared. I had been a serious question

1

asker up until then, and I wasn't sure I could change.

"I brought you into this world," I said, pointing my finger at her, "and I can take you out. If I want your advice, I'll ask for it."

Her white paws raised in surrender. "Whatever," she mumbled.

I turned my back on her, but before I left the room, I swirled around and added, "And take my dance costume off!"

It took some negotiation, but for the most part I won. Eventually, Dainy was perfect—I'd dreamed her up that way. We played dolls, plastic horses, paper cut-outs, Old Maid (she cheated) and Checkers. Dainy listened to my complaints and gave me the thumbs-up when I needed it. She made her appearances timely and knew exactly when to vanish. I was in complete control. She did anything I asked and usually took the blame when we found ourselves in trouble. My parents knew about Dainy but they didn't worry; they encouraged my creative imagination. They did not, however, go so far as to set an extra place at the table for her. They knew that I knew she was make-believe. In other words, I wasn't crazy.

Mom and I had walked a few blocks every Sunday morning to the Christian Park Reformed Church, even though my grandmother, who lived upstairs, had wanted her to go to a church for Jehovah's Witnesses called a Kingdom Hall. For reasons of her own, Mom refused. After Grandma went to heaven, or at least I thought that's where she'd gone, Mom cried a lot and reconsidered her religious viewpoints, regretting that she hadn't accompanied her mother. I vowed never to make *that* mistake! I'd follow my mom to any church she wanted. I soon discovered, however, that Mom couldn't answer any of my questions like Grandma had. She'd read scriptures from the Bible which solved my everyday problems.

One day, there came a knock at our front door and Dainy and I rushed to see who our visitors might be. Mom opened the door to a couple of nicely dressed Jehovah's Witnesses who introduced themselves as Bill and Jeannette Hastings. I'd seen them before—they'd been friends of my grandmother.

Before the interruption, Dainy and I had been cutting out paper dolls in my room. She tugged on the sleeve of my blouse, beckoning me to return to our play, but I stayed with Mom, curious to see what Bill and Jeannette would say.

Jeanette Hastings asked my mother if she had any questions about the Bible.

"Well, yes I do," Mom said. "My daughter here, has been asking questions for which I have no answers. Nor does my minister. His explanation that life is a mystery doesn't satisfy this little girl."

Dainy groaned and muttered, "Uh-oh," but no one seemed to notice.

I have no idea what question a five-year-old could ask for which a response would be so difficult, but apparently it was one of those meaning-of-life inquiries little kids have at one time or another. Perhaps I had asked, "Why am I here?" and it freaked my mother out. I don't think she knew why *she* was here.

As I was standing next to Mom, Jeannette politely turned her attention to me and smiled. She was a short, thick lady with orange-red hair wound tightly into a braided knot at the nape of her neck. She patted the top of my head and nodded meaningfully—she could satisfy my mother's pressing need for clarification. What a relief!

Bill Hastings suggested they study the Bible in our home. Mom said yes—just like that! The couple turned toward our driveway and waved in a handful of people waiting in a station wagon. I stared in wonderment as they swarmed and claimed every chair and couch cushion we owned, like at the carnival where everyone scurries around to pick the best seat on the Tilt-a-Whirl.

"We're outnumbered!" Dainy squealed. "What did I tell you? You've gone and done it now."

I ran to our sofa and jumped on for dear life. Dainy squeezed in next to me. I looked around the room and recognized a lady who'd spoken to me at Grandma's funeral. They must've all been friends of my grandmother and I figured she'd sent them to us.

Grandpa died when I was six months old and Grandma had lived with us ever since. I'd been blessed to spend a good amount of time with her. Bill and Jeannette had picked her up for church meetings, which is undoubtedly why Mom felt comfortable inviting them in as quickly as she did.

So there I sat, a five-year-old, right smack-dab in the middle of *The Truth*. Bill and Jeannette taught us that Jehovah's Witnesses were the only group that had it. Exclusively! Not Catholics, Baptists, Jews or Buddhists. Period. Jehovah God, Creator of Heaven and Earth, and the father of Jesus Christ, gave explicit direction to the entire human race through the Watchtower Bible & Tract Society, also known as the *Organization*. They could explain *everything*. They had, and they were, The Truth.

Before they left that day, they said they'd come back next week, if that was okay with Mom. I peeked through our living room window curtain as they walked away. Bill Hastings wore a dark-colored Sunday-go-to-meeting suit and a heavy overcoat. A plaid hat covered his curly salt-and-pepper hair. I'd seen men dress like this at our church, but it might be a problem for my dad if we decided to join this religion. I'd never seen anything but cuffed, long pants and white shirts in his closet, and his white shirts weren't the dressy type. I was quite familiar with his closet contents because that's where he always hid my birthday and Christmas presents.

Bill and Jeannette brought someone different from their Kingdom Hall for our home Bible study every Monday so we'd become acquainted with others from their congregation. Each week I learned something, and our new religion had a ready-made answer for every question I thought to ask. That way, I didn't have to ponder issues for myself anymore. What I didn't know, my religion did, and soon I would know it all!

When Bill Hastings smiled, his eyes lit up and I couldn't help but smile, too. He showed us scriptures to prove that once someone was in The Truth, they were rewarded with eternal life in Paradise. And the best thing of all—they didn't have to die and go to heaven to reach that ultimate place. The Garden of Eden was coming back! Paradise on Earth—where there would never again be pain, sickness, sorrow or death. Grandpa and Grandma would be resurrected and we'd all be together again. With that for a prize, who *wouldn't* want to be in The Truth?

CHAPTER TWO
THE HAPPY PEOPLE

"Very little is needed to make a happy life; it is all within yourself, in your way of thinking." ~Marcus Aurelius

After four months of home Bible studies, Bill and Jeannette decided we were ready for a public meeting. The first one we attended was in an old storefront building on East Washington Street in Indianapolis. Our mentors escorted us and held the door open as we entered. We climbed a dusty flight of steps and Dainy ran ahead, skipping two steps at a time. The place smelled inviting—like an antique shop mingled with aging newspapers and perfumes. I could hardly wait to reach the top where I discovered a long, narrow room with wood floors. Metal folding chairs were set up in rows on either side with a wide aisle in the middle. There must have been fifty people there, some already seated and others standing, engrossed in animated conversations. The auditorium vibrated with joy. We were introduced to people we hadn't met, and I noticed what appeared to be genuine smiles on their faces.

"What's everyone so happy about?" Dainy said. I'd noticed it, too, so I asked Jeannette.

"Jehovah's people are a *happy* people," she explained.

They sure were friendly, I had to give them that, and for the most part they were sincerely happy, especially delighted to meet newly interested people.

I took my seat. Dainy threw herself like a ragdoll on the chair next to mine. "These metal chairs are hard and cold," she whined.

"It's no worse than those wooden pews at the church where Mom took us before," I whispered. I craned my neck, looking for the nursery. If she didn't behave, I'd have to send her there. We were instructed to stand and sing song number 69, *Tell It Out,* from the Witness songbook: *Songs to Jehovah's Praise*. Someone in the row behind us handed Mom an extra copy and she held it so I could see it, too, even though I couldn't yet read the words or the music. I put my arm in Mom's and we smiled at one another. Dainy frowned and defiantly folded her arms across her chest, remaining seated in her cold, hard chair. *Let her pout*, I thought.

"Tell it out among the nations that our God is King. Tell it out, tell it

out."

I liked the snappy rhythm of that song. A prayer was offered and we sat down again. As the meeting progressed, I heard a baby cry and I discovered that Jehovah's Witnesses kept their children with them during the meetings—there was no nursery. I liked that practice—children were treated with respect and were expected to learn The Truth right along with their parents. That's the way I saw it then, back in 1954. As the years passed, I remained oblivious to the physical, emotional and sexual abuse many young ones suffered at the hands of elders or even their own parents. The Organization's policy was to keep it hush-hush so no reproach would be brought upon Jehovah and his "happy" people. Much later, after I'd left The Truth, I was appalled to discover what really went on and is continuing to this very day.

CHAPTER THREE
WILL SHE OR WON'T SHE?

I actually listened to the program at that first public meeting. I didn't understand everything, but I loved what I heard and the sincerity with which it was delivered. They answered questions I hadn't even thought to ask yet.

Our public meeting attendance was sporadic for months. Mom, Dad and I spent summer weekends at our two-room cabana on the banks of Brandywine Creek in Shelby County, a forty-five minute trip from our Indianapolis home. We'd usually travel to the cabin on Friday evenings and stay through late Sunday afternoon. Driving back and forth to Indianapolis for a Sunday meeting was out of the question.

Uncle Howard, my dad's brother, and Aunt Sarah joined us most weekends with my three cousins. A variety of other aunts, uncles and cousins from both sides of the family joined in the fun. Family friends showed up, too. We never really knew for sure whom we'd see driving down the long dirt road toward our cabin after we awakened on Saturday mornings. Sometimes I invited my favorite Stratford Avenue girlfriend, Susie Bechtel, when I knew a cousin or two wouldn't be there to play with. If I had no one else, there was always Dainy.

Mom and I occasionally drove the short distance from the cabin to Shelbyville for Sunday meetings where the congregation met in a garage off the alley, behind a member's house. I liked meeting in a garage—so clandestine and quiet. I had never been one to approve of the place that pomp and circumstance held in religious church services—a trick to stir people's emotions up so they'd drop more coins into collection plates. Jehovah's Witnesses didn't even pass a collection plate; they kept a "contribution box" in the rear so you'd pass it on the way out. *Clever*, I thought, *and tactful at the same time.*

By then, I was enrolled in Christian Park Public School #82, but some of my neighbor girlfriends weren't in my class. They had their own school for Catholics only. I was curious and wondered what Catholics were all about. One Sunday in particular, Mom gave me a choice and I attended Mass in Shelbyville with my Aunt Sarah and my cousin Tracey. My aunt was a loyal Catholic who hated to skip Mass. Neither Mom nor I were bonafide Jehovah's Witnesses yet; we were allowed to go to other churches. That changes the instant a person is baptized, I found out later.

7

So there I was in a Catholic cathedral. Stand up—sit down. Kneel. Stand up—sit down. Kneel. Bow your head, sing a hymn. Sit still while the priest monotonously sing-songs in Latin. I examined the stained glass window designs and eyed ladies' hats. I slid down in the pew, humiliated, with a white Kleenex bobby-pinned onto the top of my head. Tracey wore a tissue too, but she acted like it was normal.

I thought about the tiny garage across town. If I'd chosen to go there with Mom I'd have at least learned something about the Bible. I could see her now—raising her hand, being called on and answering a question aloud during the Watchtower Study. She read her lesson on Saturday afternoons, creek-side at our picnic table, where she underlined the answers with a Schaeffer fountain ink pen. The questions were found at the bottom of the page, usually one or two per paragraph. The overseer read the questions and the congregation members raised their hands if they wanted to offer an answer. Mom always seemed comfortable commenting in that little garage and I liked hearing her voice.

I confronted her one day. "Why do you answer in this meeting, but back home you don't?"

"Well . . . it's a smaller group and I'm more at ease with the casual feeling."

"I think you should start commenting at our own congregation. Do you want to be in Paradise or not?"

Apparently she'd never actually thought this whole thing through. "Really? You think I should?" I nodded fervently. From then on, we rarely missed a meeting, and there were five each week: Two in a row on Sunday morning, one on Tuesday and two on Thursday evening. I liked everything about this happy religion and wanted to *belong* to it. If Mom would make a commitment, I would follow.

CHAPTER FOUR
COMMITMENT

The belief system of one's parents is oftentimes a mandatory ritual for the child. Buck Owens sang the song "Old Time Religion" with his own rendition of lyrics: *It was good enough for mother and it was good enough for papa, it was good enough for sister and it's good enough for me.*

Grown-up children tend to blame their parental upbringing for their own bad judgment and mistakes. It seems, however, that I have no one to blame but myself. I can't even point the finger at Dainy! I did it on purpose; I'm the one who had questions, and I'm the one who encouraged my mother to take a stand—*do something!*

Mom found meaningful solutions in this home Bible class. She was baptized when I was eight. I followed up the rear and Dad, a pack of cigarettes with the famous camel logo on the front showing through the pocket of his shirt, lounged silently at the sidelines. Dainy was generally silent, too, but there were times I had to bite my tongue to keep her that way. I wonder how my life would've been different if I'd heeded her warning about religion with a capital R.

It didn't seem right to me that Jehovah would mandatorily destroy people I knew and loved. There wasn't anyone, from my cousins to my Stratford Avenue girlfriends, who I wanted to see die at Armageddon. It made my heart ache to think that strangers would be killed, too. Was this The Truth? Would God really do such a thing to innocent people?

While at a Shrine Circus with my Uncle Paul and my cousin Marsha, a clown climbed up a high stack of boxes and fell to his death. The audience gasped, but everyone speculated it was part of his act . . . until he failed to get up. An ambulance pulled into the arena and two men with a stretcher carried him out. He was covered from head to toe with a white sheet. The circus continued and I cried, wishing he'd been a Jehovah's Witness.

I vividly recall a conversation I had with Mom before her baptism.

"Are you absolutely, positively sure this is The Truth?"

"I've researched it," Mom said, "and I'm convinced, or else I would've never made a dedication. I only wish I could've known The Truth when my mom and dad were living."

I paused just long enough so she wouldn't think I wanted to argue. "It just seems so weird that I've been lucky enough to have been almost born into it without really trying. Why would Jehovah have chosen me? Am I special, or what?"

"You're worthy—look at you, how sincere you are," Mom said. "No, I have no doubts at all and neither should you."

Well.

If it was good enough for her and my grandparents, it was good enough for me. I couldn't imagine that I would ever give any thought to leaving The Truth.

Grandpa had been a Jehovah's Witness, too, but I knew him only through photographs and my mother's descriptions, which were always complimentary. In fact, I can't recall her ever complaining about anyone. She wished she could've been more like her father. I wondered why she didn't realize she was perfect the way she was.

"What was it about your dad that you'd want to be like?" I said.

"He was so patient and kind to everyone. He must have been the nicest man on earth."

I made a sound. "I don't see how *you* could be more patient and kind yourself!"

I often wished I'd had my mother's qualities of practicality and patience. She was never known to rush into a decision. She wanted to be completely certain that what she'd found was The Truth. She studied every week with Bill and Jeannette for three years before making a commitment with water baptism. From then on, she never faltered, down to the day she took her last breath one week before her eighty-first birthday, over forty years of faithful service. I was proud of her because that's what she wanted —to be faithful to the end, whether at her death, or at Armageddon which would usher in Paradise on Earth. Mom trusted the JW teaching that after a faithful one dies, they are asleep, awaiting a resurrection once Jehovah has destroyed all evil, thrown Satan into the abyss, and brought the Earth back to the paradise condition of the original Garden of Eden.

CHAPTER FIVE
THE TRUTH

*"I don't know exactly when I started falling out of The Truth,
but I remember the precise moment when, way up high in a
tree, I made the decision to get in." ~ from Chapter Six*

I swear to tell the truth, the whole truth, and nothing but the truth. So what is The Truth?

It wasn't difficult to join. Typically, an adult—I'll call him Harold Householder—reads Bible-based literature left at his door by Joe Publisher. He questions what he's read, and Joe Publisher provides satisfactory answers, thanks to his training from the Organization. Along Harold's journey, he is advised to use only the New World Translation of the Bible, translated and published by the Organization, so as not to be confused with the antiquated English of the King James Version or other inferior translations. Harold attends five meetings a week at the local Kingdom Hall and finally decides to make the oath and take the plunge that will put him in The Truth.

However, he must wait for an assembly of JWs for that to happen, where he'll seat himself along with a large group of people, awaiting water baptism. After a thirty-minute lecture, the group will be asked a two-part question: "On the basis of the sacrifice of Jesus Christ, have you repented of your sins and dedicated yourself to Jehovah to do his will, and do you understand that your dedication and baptism identify you as one of Jehovah's Witnesses in association with *God's spirit-directed organization."* They will all answer with an unequivocal YES! The audience will cheer and clap in solidarity, a prayer to Jehovah will be offered, and the baptismal candidates will don their modest bathing attire (no bikinis, two-pieces or Speedos) and be led to an immersion pool.

After being fully submerged in water, Harold will officially be in The Truth! Most likely, Joe Publisher will be in the audience, feeling so proud of Harold—and of himself, too. Everyone in the congregation will pat Joe on the back because, after all, he helped bring Harold Householder into The Truth!

But wait! Once you're baptized, there's no turning back. Woe be to Harold if he ever changes his mind!

11

CHAPTER SIX
I CAN'T SAY DAINY DIDN'T WARN ME

"I was so naïve as a child I'd hide behind the barn and do nothing." ~Johnny Carson

I simplified Harold's experience, and while it may be typical, that's not the way it happened to me. I don't know exactly when I started falling out of The Truth, but I remember the precise moment when, way up high in a tree, I made the decision to get in. I did it on purpose—the choice was entirely my own.

In the six years that followed that first encounter at our front door, I'd attended over sixteen-hundred meetings and two dozen Circuit and District Conventions where I observed the baptism routine—the two questions answered in the affirmative. I knew the drill.

At the age of eleven, I impulsively decided that baptism might be a good thing for me. I reached the verdict after a breezy Friday evening in June, during an open-air Circuit Assembly at the Shelby County Fairgrounds. An announcement that the immersion process would take place the following afternoon caught my attention. "Friends," the speaker implored, revival style. "Search your hearts. Any one of you who feels compelled to dedicate their life to Jehovah God should prayerfully consider baptism tomorrow!"

Hey, that sounds like a terrific idea! I thought. The following afternoon, Saturday, June 6, 1959, I was dunked into a lake and dedicated my life to Paradise . . . I mean, Jehovah God.

Mom and I had already packed our overnight bags with dresses to wear to the assembly. A good wife in the 1950's would ask her husband's permission, rather than simply say, "I'm taking the station wagon into town for the day." My parents, however, were a peaceful couple and didn't seem to have rules by which to play; they were on the same team—Team Joanna, I liked to think. I often heard Dad tell Mom whatever she wanted was fine with him. He didn't mind that we drove fifteen miles to Shelbyville and back for what seemed important to us. He drove that route two or three times each weekend for a six-pack. I noticed he'd stocked up from home with a case of beer this time, and if that didn't hold him, our visitors usually brought extras.

In Biblical times, Laodicea was a city in Asia Minor whose Christians were rebuked for their indifference to religion. (Revelation 3:16) Dad, whose ancestors may have originated in Laodicea, forever remained apathetic to religion of any kind, even though we invited him to accompany us on a regular basis. Mom and I didn't like the thought of living in a Paradise Earth without him.

Occasionally, on rainy days at our cabin, Dainy took the form of an upside-down mop. I braided the strands of her hair, tied the ends with pink ribbons, and we danced throughout the little two-room cabana. On sunny days, I loved climbing trees down by the creek. I guess I was a tree hugger from an early age. I always took my imaginary Dainy with me and we had the most enlightening conversations in thick, leafy branches, hidden away from the view of anyone down below.

On the weekend in question, early Saturday morning, we'd climbed up an oak tree and discussed my epiphany from the night before. A spur-of-the-moment decision—my baptism—not pre-meditated in any way. There we were, way up high, and Dainy suddenly went off to a world of her own and was of no help to me! She refused to offer her opinion one way or the other, so what was I to do?

I decided to ask The Man himself; I wrote Him a note.

> Dear Jehovah, Do you think I should get baptized?
> Yes_____ No_____
> Please answer by Noon.

I folded and placed it inside a tiny cardboard ring box. Mom called me to breakfast; I swore Dainy to secrecy and left her in the tree to watch over things for me while I was gone. That was the least she could do.

I descended, leaving the ultimate verdict in the capable hands of God Almighty. I could hardly wait until noon for an answer, and yet I'd give Jehovah the time He needed to make up His mind; He was a very busy Creator.

At noon on the dot, I shimmied back up the tree and eagerly opened the box. I expected one of the answers to have some kind of a mark on it, at least a smudge or a crease line.

I gasped. "What's this? He didn't check yes *or* no!"

"He didn't show up," Dainy said in a monotone.

"Oh, yes he did," I hissed. "He was here all right. You just can't see Him.

What to do now? I sighed. "Well . . . He didn't say NO. That, in itself, must be a sign."

Dainy wore a smirk, a know-it-all expression I'd seen before. "Do you realize these people don't believe dinosaurs were real? They say it's a scientific hoax."

"It probably is, then."

"What about Susie and Joanie, back home on Stratford Avenue? You're okay with leaving them behind to die at Armageddon?"

I ignored her and made her stay in the tree while I slid down and informed my mother that I would take my swimsuit to the assembly for the baptism. Her mouth literally fell open. "Oh. Well. Sure. Ah . . . ." Then, she smiled. "Why, that's a *wonderful* idea," she said, once the concept had soaked in. It had taken her three years to make such a commitment, yet her daughter had decided overnight. Mom continued smiling behind the steering wheel all the way to Shelbyville.

I had made her happy. I vowed right then and there to keep right on making my mother happy because I liked the effect on her. She'd been rather gloomy that morning; Dad had been plastered, as usual on Friday evening, passed out early, then awakened before daybreak on Saturday, marching around the cabin whacking an aluminum saucepan with a metal spoon, shouting "Reveille!" I'd do anything to make her smile—I would never disappoint my mother, I thought.

I listened as carefully as any eleven-year old can listen to the sermon given prior to the immersion. Brother A. J. Manera had been sent directly from Society Headquarters in New York to oversee the assembly.

Manera's amplified voice boomed into the microphone to emphasize the importance of what we were doing there. Soon, it was time for the crucial two-part question. "Have you repented of your sins?" I knew I had to answer in the affirmative, but right after the first question I turned to the person beside me with the urge to ask, "Hey, wait! What does that mean?" But, he looked as confused as I felt. I couldn't think of any sins I'd committed yet, so I wasn't sure if I should confess to them anyway. *If only Dainy were here*, I thought. Well, whatever it meant, I was sure it was okay to answer YES! because everyone else was saying it right out loud. "YES! YES!" they shouted. I'd dedicated my life to Jehovah in that oak tree and I was ready to see it through.

I wondered how many others had made this resolution within the past few hours as I had done. Did anyone ever murmur "no" under their breath? No one would hear them if they did, but Jehovah would know. *He knew everything.*

After the prayer, we were escorted out while everyone else sang "Dedication," song number seventy-four. We headed to a bath house with cold, concrete floors and changed into our swim wear. While trailing down the hill to the lake, I overheard a woman's voice behind me. "They baptize 'em at any age, don't they?" She obviously did not approve of my youthful ability to make a vital decision. I mulled it over, waited about thirty seconds, then turned to see what she looked like. There were two of them—wrinkled old ladies—at least fifty years old. I was inclined to sneer and loudly proclaim, "Why should my age be any of your business? I want to serve the Creator of Heaven and Earth just as you do!" However, I turned around and marched straight ahead. I made a conscious choice not to say a word, but if Dainy had been with me there would've been a scene. Isn't it odd that after all of these years I still remember the raw, hurtful feeling a woman's disapproval evoked in me? I recently read a valuable quote, "What others think of us is none of our business." If only I'd known that then!

While I waited in line on the sandy beach, I watched others going under water. When their legs popped back up and they weren't completely immersed, back down they went. Sometimes it took two brothers to hold them under. That wouldn't happen to me, I thought. I wasn't afraid of going under water because I did it all the time in Brandywine Creek. Uncle Howard had taught me to swim a long time ago.

Then it was my turn. The brother had me pinch my nose with my right hand and cross my left arm over to hold my right wrist, then he put one hand under my head and the other one on my folded arms. On my way down, I pretended I was holding Jehovah's hand. I thought, *Here we go, Jehovah. This is it.* He would be my invisible friend from now until eternity. I probably wouldn't need Dainy any longer. I knew what I was doing—I did it on purpose and with resolve.

CHAPTER SEVEN
FALLING OUT OF THE TRUTH

"If people are good only because they fear punishment, and hope for reward, then we are a sorry lot indeed." ~ Albert Einstein

Jehovah's Witnesses didn't believe in a "once saved, always saved" doctrine. Baptism didn't wash sins away or save you from Hell or anything. It's only a symbol, they said. My immersion symbolized my dedication to Jehovah and my belief that the Watchtower Bible and Tract Society was *the* one, the *only* organization He used. I now belonged; I was in The Truth!

We didn't return to the fairgrounds for the Sunday portion of the assembly. Mom had been baptized for three years and I was fresh out of the lake, so we figured we were safe to miss one meeting. Plus, Mom thought it wouldn't be proper to leave my dad two days in a row at the cabin, so I had the privilege of parading around my cousins, boasting that I was now baptized!

I had not yet heard the term "falling out of The Truth" and I knew nothing of being *disfellowshipped*—kicked out! Those were only two of many Jehovah's Witness teachings that came into question later.

I'm unsure why they use the terminology "falling out" because one never just *falls* out. A good thing too, because since I'd made the decision to get in while fifteen feet off the ground, can you imagine the damage I would've done to myself if I'd have dropped from the same distance?

Let's use Harold Householder to illustrate. Harold misses meetings, one after the other, until he quits going altogether. If you stop eating food, you become physically sick, and so it is with spirituality, according to the Organization. Harold stops feeding upon the Watchtower publications and Harold is oh so spiritually sick!

Or, perhaps Harold is *stumbled* by someone, what they said—what they did—and he stomps off—away from the Organization—his ego in charge. Possibly Harold commits adultery, or smokes cigarettes, lies, cheats or steals, and rather than show a repentant attitude, he becomes defensive, refusing to stop this sinful behavior.

Consider this simplified scenario: What if Harold simply changes his mind and wants to practice his spirituality outside of organized religion? God forbid.

Remember Joe Publisher, the one who brought Harold into The Truth? He does everything short of a rain dance to turn Harold around, but nothing works. For whatever reason, Harold is disillusioned and won't get back in line. The elders have no choice but to pow-wow and elect to kick Harold out in order to protect the cleanliness of the entire congregation.

An announcement is made at the conclusion of the Service Meeting on Thursday evening that Harold is now DISFELLOWSHIPPED! While Joe sits forlornly in his chair, severely disappointed in his protégé, others in the congregation stiffen, bracing themselves for the worst. They can no longer have anything to do with Harold Householder. Too bad if his entire family is in the Organization—Harold just lost his family and all the "true" friends he ever had. Everyone now pats Joe Publisher on the back and offers their condolences. They know how he must feel—like a failure, a *loser*.

Of course, Harold is the real loser because he is no longer to be rewarded with everlasting life in Paradise. Tsk. Tsk. But, there is always hope. A disfellowshipped sinner can qualify for salvation and forgiveness, followed by reinstatement into the congregation. If he has a change of heart, Harold can show repentance and jump through a few hoops. A number of people I knew during my long stint in The Truth sought reinstatement only to reacquire the company of their family and friends. I, too, personally experienced this phenomenon, which I explain in Chapter Thirty-Seven: *I Want My Mother Back!* While I chose ultimately to leave the Organization for good, some remain for the rest of their days, with very little enthusiasm.

The Organization frequently changes its viewpoint on doctrine, but a member who reconsiders his own method of worship is frowned upon. But that's exactly what I did: I reevaluated my life because my religion had become a roadblock to my spirituality. I left with the identical resolve I had when I entered. I'd made a life-altering decision up in a tree as a child, and with both feet on the ground I made an equally significant one four decades later.

CHAPTER EIGHT
YOU MUST SET BOUNDARIES, YOU KNOW

Back then, congregations were named according to locality, as is the continued practice today. Ours was Irvington, and while we lived in the Christian Park neighborhood, Irvington was a little community nearby. Sometimes the boundary lines were changed, thus a congregation might lose and gain a few members. One evening I was thrilled to see a new girl at our meeting. I was ten years old and she appeared close to my age. I walked right up to her and said hello. Her name was Susan Spencer. She lived only a few blocks from me, but we'd never met. She attended Public School #56.

Susan and I became instant friends and we remained close, seeing each other through marriages, children and grandchildren. I've called her several times since I left the Organization in 1997. She has my telephone number and promised to call, but she hasn't. She didn't accept my friend request on Facebook. It's obvious she's made her choice, and I don't pursue her any further. I'm not the stalking type. You think you have lifetime friends in the Organization? Try leaving.

Eventually we moved from the storefront building to a real Kingdom Hall. The brothers had volunteered their weekends for over a year and built a new meeting place for Irvington. Additionally, a new unit had been formed, boundaries re-worked again. Susan and I sat on the edge of our seats as they read off the names of those who would stay with Irvington and those who would go with the new group. What a relief to discover we would still be together in the Christian Park Congregation!

Witnesses had black and white rules for everything. It was unacceptable to attend a congregation outside of your boundary. If you did it anyway, you were probably spiritually sick or there was something wrong with you. You definitely weren't in the mainstream, that's for sure.

We would share the Hall with the East Unit, having our Ministry School and Service Meetings on Thursday, while East met on Friday night. We held a Public Talk and Watchtower Study on Sunday afternoon and attended in smaller groups in private homes for the Book Study on Tuesday evening. When I walked into that little Hall on Brookside Drive for the first time, Dainy said, "What is that smell?" The scent was a unique one, and I can distinctly recall it but find no suitable words to portray it other than *calming*. It was as though someone had cooked a pot of butternut squash soup with an extra portion of fresh ginger and brown sugar. Week after week, the aroma relaxed my soul. It embraced me, wrapped a secure sensation around me. It always settled me no matter what kind of day I'd had. I knew I was protected there, and this was the Kingdom Hall I would eventually be married in years later.

CHAPTER NINE
WHO'S THAT KNOCKING ON MY DOOR?

I knocked on the front door, my book bag by my side, ready to present two magazines for ten cents.

"It's just a shame," the lady scolded, no sooner than she'd cracked her door open. "It's wrong for them religious people to send you to collect money like this!" I wondered why she believed we made any money off a five-cent magazine. Besides, that's not the way it was at all. I enjoyed talking to people. I had a message of everlasting life, and if they'd listen to me as the messenger, they'd live forever in Paradise. Who wouldn't want something like that? I knew I sure did. As soon as Mom and I got the picture from that group of people she studied with about the future we could have, we had only one question: Where do we sign up?

During my youth, I walked door-to-door with all sorts of people from our congregation and occasionally from others. I achieved my education in human behavior and weirdness while out in the ministry work. We preached in the poor projects and the richest of neighborhoods. I sat on sofas with cock roaches running around on the floors, snotty-nosed babies climbing all over me, and dogs and cats jumping on my lap. Of course these were in the poor neighborhoods, because the rich rarely invited us in. They already had the solutions to their problems. The poor were the humble ones. I quickly learned not to be judgmental of the poor. I saw how difficult their lives were which helped me appreciate what I had in my life.

Adult publishers would say to me, "What a zealous little publisher you are!" I couldn't wait to show off the magazines; I told everyone who'd listen that these magazines would change their life if they'd read them, and if they had kids with questions—well here are your answers! Many householders handed over their ten cent contribution because they couldn't resist an enthusiastic little girl with bright blue eyes and dimples. I'd brag upon re-entering the car about how many magazines I'd placed, and the grownups would say, "Oh you're such a cute kid, who could resist you?" If my dimples helped magazine sales, it was okay with me, because I was sure once those journals ended up on their coffee tables, the householders would sit down and flip open the pages and, before they knew it, they'd be delighted to find they could live forever if only they followed the rules. And who wouldn't want to live forever? I couldn't imagine anyone not wanting to. It was the ultimate answer to any little kid's questions about where we come from and where we are going and why we have to die—you know... *those* types of questions.

I'd found my calling in the ministry work—I would help other people learn how to live forever!

CHAPTER TEN
TELL IT OUT AMONG THE NATIONS

Within a few months after my baptism, the Organization opened up the Ministry School to women. This meant the sisters could give five-minute "talks" from the platform, although not addressing the audience directly, but sitting down across from another sister (a householder type), as though in conversation. I signed up right away.

We were taught to create an *introduction* that would arouse interest; a *body* that would explain the Bible's view of a specific issue; and a *conclusion*, summarizing our theme.

I received my first talk assignment and Mom helped me develop the theme and setting. My householder was Peggy Huber, a girl with brown curly hair who giggled a lot. We visited her and rehearsed thoroughly until I was satisfied Peggy would say her part on cue. I'd memorized the entire thing. I waited for the big day and practiced over and over. I had it timed down to the second, but I hadn't imagined how nervous I would be once I was up on the platform in front of the entire congregation. I talked so fast there was still one minute left on the Ministry School Overseer's stopwatch after I finished! I kept reminding myself that I was merely the messenger and the audience wasn't really looking at *me*. My delivery as the messenger was equally as important in the Ministry School as it was when I went out in service. If I delivered the ideas properly, the audience would learn from my words.

Each speaker had a counsel slip, and every time I'd give a talk, the overseer would mark a G for *Good*, an S for *Satisfactory* or a W for *Work on this*. These points of counsel were for such things as setting, introduction, body development, conclusion, gestures, illustrations or timing. I usually merited a "G" but I don't think I ever gave a talk when afterward I wasn't admonished to SLOW DOWN. Every time I'd have rehearsed it right at five minutes, but because of nervousness I talked so fast the entire thing would be over in three minutes! I wrote "SLOW" all over the margins of my notes until I finally learned to relax and develop good public speaking habits.

I give the Ministry School credit for my ability to communicate with others in such a way that they listen to what I am saying. I've stifled yawns during talks that had the most boring of settings with a generic theme, such as talking to another sister who was depressed, or who had a question about the meaning of a scripture. The majority of my beloved sisters had no imagination whatsoever. My least favorite lead-in was this: "Are you ready for your Bible study, Sister Jones?" Ugh. I sat through those talks imagining what those women did for entertainment. Did they eat chocolates while watching soap operas, shop downtown at fine places like Wasson's and L. S. Ayres, or did they stay at home polishing hardwood floors and dusting coffee tables? I would've bet money on the latter if gambling hadn't been against my religion.

It was important for me to create attention-grabbing settings. My setting would be the first thing people saw or heard and would arouse their curiosity. Later as an adult when I developed an interest in fiction writing, I understood the first sentence—the first paragraph—of a short story or novel must be the *hook*. If the readers weren't hooked, they wouldn't care about the rest.

I developed my skills, concluding my little speech like tying a bow around a gift, producing a whole and satisfying package. I've read novels that were fascinating until the very end, when the author fizzled out and I was left wanting a grand finale! What a disappointment and waste of time reading a book of that kind, and I rarely purchased another of those authors' books.

The Ministry School was my early education in communicating through the written word and verbally. Presentation was the key. I learned to present my ideas within a five-minute timeframe which would come in handy later as an adult in the business world. Since the Organization highly discouraged college, at least I received that much of an education from The Truth!

CHAPTER ELEVEN
SHOPPING FOR BOYS

Around the age of thirteen, Susan Spencer and I decided to walk casually around the auditorium during a Circuit Assembly intermission. We were interested in meeting people, specifically boys, although Susan was shy and I was the one who found it necessary to start conversations.

Dainy still followed me, though not as much as when I was younger. It was at this assembly where Dainy exclaimed, "Whoa, don't look now. Well . . . maybe you'd better. Okay, take a look at that, would ya?"

I was already looking. In the orchestra pit sat a boy tuning his violin. He wore an odd combination of plaid pants and a striped shirt underneath a sport jacket. The reason Dainy noticed him, other than his unusual wardrobe choice, is because he was rather scrawny. For some reason I was always attracted to the runts because my grandfather and my dad were both little guys, so I was most comfortable with a male of that stature. If I had to tilt my head up to see his face, I could never find an attraction, even if I tried. I needed to look him right in the eyes! So, I watched this boy throughout the weekend, but in spite of Dainy's urgings, I couldn't find the nerve to talk to him.

I pointed him out to my mother during the meeting and she strained her head sideways to take a peek at him. Then, she raised her eyebrows and leaned closer toward me. "What's his name?" she whispered.

"I don't know," I said, "but I know I like him!"

Mom smiled.

We had two circuit assemblies each year, usually six months apart. At the next assembly I watched for that boy and sure enough, there he was in the orchestra. I wouldn't call it stalking, but I did follow him from a distance to see if I could meet him but I still couldn't find the courage. Once I made a point to walk right past him, but he didn't notice that I existed. I made a vow to myself that at the next assembly I would make it happen. Somehow, Dainy and I would think of something!

CHAPTER TWELVE
MEETING BOBBY

*"I bought angora in ten different shades and wore Bobby's
ring with the fuzzy yarn wrapped around it for the world to
see." ~ Chapter Thirteen*

An announcement was made at our congregation. Another unit was to
be formed, boundaries once again adjusted, and we would meet with the East
Unit the following week to determine the status. *Well, that's going to be
crowded*, I thought, and I told Mom we'd better arrive early so we could park
in the small lot behind the hall. She didn't like to park on Brookside Drive
because of its shabby, inner-city feel. I walked into the foyer, took a whiff of
the familiar scent and went to find our seats. I heard Dainy say, "Don't look
now . . . ." Of course, I looked. What a surprise when I saw the boy—THE
boy! I garnered two seats, three rows behind his family so I could stare at
him without anyone suspecting. His father stood up to give a talk and was
introduced as Robert Lufcy. I figured since his son appeared to be his oldest
child, I'd think of him as Bobby. I couldn't believe my luck! And to think, all
this time we'd been attending the same hall, only on different days of the
week.

"We've probably sat in the same chair as he has more than a time or
two, don't you imagine?" Dainy said. That sent a little shiver down my spine,
don't think it didn't.

An announcement was made that the Irvington Congregation had
moved into their brand new Kingdom Hall. Furthermore, the East
Congregation would now be the Brookside Unit. Family names were read out
loud, and only some minor adjustments were made, leaving the Lufcy family
at Brookside and Mom and me at Christian Park. *Drats!* I thought.

The Christian Park Unit had purchased some land five blocks from our
house on Stratford Avenue and would begin construction on a new hall.
Wow, I thought, *we can walk to the meetings if we want.* Unfortunately, that
project took over seven years due to its intricate design and the reliance on
volunteer carpenters who eventually tired of spending all their weekends on
the architectural disaster, I was told. By the time it was finished, I was twenty
and married, living in Greenfield, Indiana.

After that joint meeting with East and Christian Park, someone

25

introduced me to the boy, and sure enough he was Robert Lufcy, Jr., known as Bobby to everyone. Dainy raised one eyebrow and winked proudly at me, since I'd already named him Bobby in my mind.

I developed friendships with two teenage girls at the Brookside Unit—Sherry Cornett and Linda Combest. Occasionally I'd go to their Friday night meeting and we'd have a sleepover afterwards. Linda's family occupied the entire upstairs of an old building, and the rooms were huge with wood floors and tall ceilings but not much light. I really liked Linda and her handful of siblings. We'd make popcorn and stay up late to watch Fright Night on the local channel from Bloomington, Indiana. I developed a friendship with Bobby that way, too, because we'd hang out after the Friday night meetings and spend time in our ministry work the following Saturday mornings. Bobby's father arranged car groups, assigning specific neighborhoods for us to cover. He always managed to make sure Linda, Sherry, and I were in Bobby's group. He knew his son liked the ladies!

Bobby had been told by my trusty friends that I liked him, but he claimed he wasn't interested. Honestly, he was the kind of boy who had a different girlfriend every month.

"Forget about him," Mom said. "He's fickle."

"What's fickle?"

"Look it up," she said.

I opened my dictionary and read that a fickle lover is not constant or loyal in his affections. I didn't care—I still liked him—there was just something about him. I made up my mind that one of these days I would be his girlfriend and I'd rock his world for a month—a month of Sundays!

CHAPTER THIRTEEN
LET'S PARTY

Bobby's sister Ladonna had a party in their back yard on a concrete patio, and I was invited! I'd never been to a Witness party before. Chef Boyardee pizza, homemade fudge and a record player were all we needed. Bryan Smith, a good friend of mine from my congregation, accompanied me. Bryan was crazy about me, but he was tall, so . . . oh well. We danced together a few times, and I danced with Susan Spencer and Linda Combest and finally, toward the end of the evening, Bobby took my hand and escorted me to the middle of the patio. A slow song had just begun. I thought I'd die! Dainy stood in the opposite corner of the patio with a look that said, "See, I told you it would happen!"

Alma Lufcy, Bobby's mother and party chaperone, apparently had put in a good word for me. I thought my knees would buckle when Bobby said, "My mother suggested I take a better look at you."

"Do you always do what your mother tells you?" I asked.

"Not always, but I did this time."

"So, what do you see?"

"The girl I've been looking for all my life." Bobby asked me to go steady.

Yes! It's about time.

Bobby kept me as his girlfriend for eight months, a record for him. All of our friends were amazed. I was pleased with my accomplishment. I bought angora in ten different shades and wore Bobby's ring with the fuzzy yarn wrapped around it for the world to see.

According to the Organization, a dating couple should never be alone because their emotions might get the best of them, and they could commit a sin in the heat of passion. A couple, young or old, should at all times be chaperoned with no exceptions, so Bobby and I were never left totally alone, but it didn't bother us. He snuck a kiss in ever-so-often. At a circuit assembly, we stood on a balcony overlooking the main auditorium and Bobby put his arm around me for a few minutes during an intermission. I loved it.

"Joanna, we need to talk," Mom said, later that day.

That didn't sound good. "About what?"

"I was informed by a dear friend, someone who cares very much about your wellbeing, that you were seen with Bobby's arm around you."

What? There were spies in our midst? "Who told you *that*!" Whoever it was, I hated her already.

"It doesn't matter who told me. What matters is that you mustn't allow a boy to show affection to you at such a young age."

"Mom! We weren't doing anything wrong. I'm nearly fourteen years old; I'm not a child anymore!"

"You weren't doing anything wrong, per se, but it gives the appearance of loose morals. You must be concerned about appearances at all times, especially at an assembly. Other young ones might see you and think they'd like to do that, too."

I shook my head. Of *course* other kids would like to do that too, but I didn't care about them. This was my private business and I was determined to find out who'd snitched on me. It could have been any number of people with good intentions, for in the Organization we were taught the scriptural command for Christians to watch each other closely and stop someone before they made a false step.

"I won't do it again, Mom. I must've known I shouldn't let him put his arm around me, because I felt guilty as soon as you said something. My brain agrees with you, but my heart wants what it wants."

"Thus the scripture, 'The human heart, who can know it.' We can't trust our emotions for guidance," Mom explained, "especially with a member of the opposite sex."

I never did find out who'd ratted on me.

~*~

I'd grown distant from my neighborhood childhood friends during my early teens, or maybe they withdrew from me. That was the way it was supposed to be, according to my religion. We were discouraged from associating with worldly people. Anyone who wasn't a Witness was considered worldly, a distraction from pure worship.

During Junior High, I was invited into the school choir. We were scheduled to perform at the historical Murat Temple in front of a large audience in December. We went beforehand for a practice, and I stood in awe of the middle-eastern and Egyptian style of architecture. I couldn't wait for our performance in front of an audience. One of our song selections was O Holy Night, but the choir director would allow me to stand silently since I didn't celebrate Christmas. My mother took it upon herself to ask the brothers about it, and they insisted I quit the choir immediately because if anyone saw me they wouldn't realize I was actually not participating in that song. We had to be conscious of how we appeared to non-believers. I was furious that my mother had felt the need to report on me. I loved to sing and hear my voice blend in with my classmates.

"We're doing things God's way, the Christian way," my mother explained, "and our reward will come in the future when we live forever on Earth. So be a good girl and be patient."

In the '60s, television advertised my Dad's favorite beer: "You only go around once in life, so you have to grab for all the gusto you can get!" Gusto, how I loved that word. I figured it was probably a sin, but I wanted my gusto *now*. The future seemed such a long time off for the reward Christians were promised. Dainy reminded me repeatedly, "At least you have a boyfriend."

Mom worked every-other-Saturday in a downtown Indianapolis doctor's office. On her way to work she dropped me off at Bobby's on a Saturday morning. We'd go out knocking on doors, then accompany his mother to three or four grocery stores in the neighborhood for which she'd cut coupons out of the newspaper. Later on those afternoons, we'd fix Chef Boyardee and sit on the front porch swing. Our relationship was pure and clean. I was happy to just sit and talk, to hear and understand a male perspective. We'd kiss and hold hands, and he'd occasionally put his arm around me on the swing, but neither of us had any interest in getting to second base. I knew Bobby was just as determined to be a person of high morals as I was.

During our meals at home, I always took my ring off and set it aside so the angora wouldn't get soiled.

My dad reached across the table and picked up the ring, holding it in the air. "How long is *this* gonna last?"

I grinned. "Bobby has never gone steady with a girl this long before—seven months now."

"What's the deal with that boy? He's way too forward for my taste."

I felt the grin melt off my face.

Mom chimed in, "He's a flatterer."

"What's that?" I sighed; it was two against one now.

"He butters me up way too much," Mom said. "Like, 'Oh, you look so beautiful today,' or 'Hello, Gorgeous!' and that sort of thing."

"Oh Mom, that's just his way of complimenting you. He doesn't mean any harm."

Dad didn't waste any time interjecting his opinion. "My bullshit meter tells me that little whippersnapper is insincere if anyone ever was. And he stands way too close to me. I don't like him."

"Gee whiz, Dad. Why don't you say what you really think?" It was true, I'd noticed Bobby's tendency to invade one's personal space, but I didn't say a word about it.

The following month Bobby broke up with me (to see other people, of course), and my parents breathed sighs of relief, even though they knew my heart was broken. But, that was temporary; I'd expected it to happen eventually. Bobby was not the boy I married, but he did introduce me to Jim.

CHAPTER FOURTEEN
HERE WE GO

The first time I saw Jim, he was walking up the aisle with a microphone attached to a cord plugged into a receptacle in the rear of the hall. This was during the Brookside Ministry School meeting, and he would pass the microphone down the row to whomever was called upon to make a comment. He wore thick glasses and had reddish hair parted on the side, way too close to his ear. I had the strongest urge to ask him for his comb so I could show him the proper way to style his hair. I leaned over to Linda Combest and said, "Who's that boy with the mic?" She whispered back, "Jim Coe."

Ah-ha, I thought. I'd heard Bobby mention Jim Coe's name a few times, but I'd never met him. He was new in the neighborhood—new in The Truth. We were both fifteen. It was unusual for a boy of his age to be given the responsibilities of handling the microphones and sound system, especially since he wasn't even baptized yet. It gave him extra points in my book. I wasted no time making his acquaintance.

I went to the Brookside meetings as often as I could after that, and Jim and I would chat after the meetings until the brothers turned out the lights and locked the door. Occasionally, we'd be in a car group together on Saturdays for ministry work, if I'd managed to finagle an invitation from Linda for a sleepover. I was impressed with Jim's sincerity about The Truth and his maturity. He wasn't like most boys his age, more serious, as though he'd been born an old man. He had definite plans for his future. Jim played the clarinet in the Circuit's orchestra at our assemblies. He refused to listen to anything but classic radio stations, determined that rock and roll was from the Devil. I always put my "Theocratic side" forward when I was around him. He didn't need to know Dainy danced the Twist with Chubby Checker in my bedroom.

One day, after spending the morning in a car group with Jim, I summoned the courage to call him from a pay phone down the street from Linda's house. I closed the door of the phone booth, but the outside temperature was no more than twenty degrees. I shook all over from the cold, but I couldn't wait to tell him how I felt about him. I wanted him to say he felt it too.

There was a long pause. "Well," Jim said, "you're a really nice girl, and you're cute, but I kinda have my sights set on someone else."

I refused to let disappointment show in my voice. "Oh really?" I said as cheerfully as I could. "Who is she?" I took a deep breath, covered the receiver with my gloves and blew out a white cloud, icing up a spot of glass on the inside of the phone booth.

The minute he said her name, I pulled off one glove and carved a check mark in the patch of frost with my fingernail. I could win that battle. The girl had no personality, no natural looks, and didn't accessorize well. She was all about The Truth, though, and that's what he must've seen in her. Two peas in a pod, those two.

"Good choice," I said, trying to sound sincere. "She's very theocratic." (*And boring*, I thought. *And ugly*.) "Have you asked her out yet?"

"Not yet."

"Well . . . is she aware you're interested in her?"

"Probably not. I'm not very forward, you know, kinda shy."

I figured my Dad would love him. "Yeah, well, that's one of the things I like about you. (*Score one for me*, I thought.) Listen, I can start dating when I turn sixteen in October, so give it some thought, and if you want to go out sometime, give me a call."

"Okay . . . I might," Jim said tentatively.

"Good. I'll talk to you then!" I hung up. *Victory is mine*, I thought.

Sure enough, Jim called a few days before my sixteenth birthday and asked me if I wanted to double-date with Bobby Lufcy and his current girlfriend at the Twin-Aire drive-in movie. *Yes!* Sitting in the back seat of Bobby's car wasn't going to be a big thrill, but I was so over him I knew I could breeze through.

I stood in our only bathroom (who had two baths in the '60's?) and fixed my hair and powdered my nose. As I looked in the mirror, Dainy said, "I always knew someday you'd stand right here and doll yourself up for our very first date. And now you're really doing it!" I grinned, happy to cross yet another milestone on my way to becoming a grown-up.

The Beatles were the rage, and on our way to the movie Bobby's radio blared with *I Want To Hold Your Hand*. I laid my hand on the seat between Jim and me, hoping he'd take the hint. He didn't.

Jim and I spent many hours on the telephone late at night, developing a solid friendship. He shared intimate details about his family and home life. He planned to move out on his own as soon as possible and I knew he could do anything he set his mind to. He was that kind of guy. I never once doubted his abilities. Whenever I had occasion to be at his house for dinner, his mother would fix an extraordinary meal, and his siblings and parents sat around a large, round maple dining table. Jim's dad's name was Jack. I passed Jack the mashed potatoes. He laughed and said, "You'd better learn how to cook because Jim loves to eat." I was embarrassed since this insinuated Jim and I would be husband and wife someday. It was a little premature, but it was Jack's way of saying he approved of me.

There were days and weeks between our phone calls or visits, and I didn't know whether or not he ever asked that other girl out. I never inquired because I didn't want him to think I cared. I didn't pressure him to be with me alone, but I made myself so enjoyable to be with that I couldn't see how he'd ever want to be with her, or anyone but me. We'd made no commitment to one another. In fact we'd never kissed. That was about to change.

Six months after our first date, a family from Jim's congregation dropped us off after the meeting at Jim's house. Jack would take me home later that night. Jim fumbled with the door key and leaned down to pick up his briefcase. On the way back up he planted a kiss on my forehead—April 3, 1964 we were officially going steady by my definition.

Jim believed wearing a high school class ring was worldly and he shunned the label of going steady. I casually mentioned the *friendship ring* principal, which signified a commitment not to date other people. He laughed at the idea. "It's a worldly fad, that's all it is." So, I bought one for myself. I wore it to school, like all my other worldly classmates. I had a love-life and I wanted the kids to know it. I wanted to *appear* normal, at least. I never showed it to Susan Spencer and I wouldn't dare wear it to the Kingdom Hall.

~*~

I'd been driving with a Beginner Driver's Permit for six months, so when I turned sixteen I was ready for my real driver's license. Dad took me to the Bureau of Motor Vehicles and when we returned home I felt like ants were crawling all over my skin. I wanted to take that car out all by myself just because I could. Dad worked second-shift and it was not yet noon, but he'd already popped the cap off a beer bottle. His eyes were alert, so maybe if he stopped with just one he'd go to work. He'd skipped work quite often since he became a member of the union. I told Dad I had "The Crave" and asked him if I could take the car a few miles to White Castle. Dad smiled a knowing smile, tossed me his car keys and said "bring one back for me—no make that two!" I drove along Washington Street, and the entire time I felt I was swerving to within one inch from the cars on either side of me. I wondered if the steering wheel had loosened. It had never felt as scary when I drove with my Beginner's Permit with someone else in the front seat beside me. The responsibility of growing up weighed heavily upon me that day, and I knew those thin, square hamburgers with their soggy buns, steamed onions, and pickle slices would cure me. Sure enough, the ride back home was easier, and I skipped in through the front door and handed Dad his car keys and a white sack with a blue castle on the front.

He tucked into his sliders and opened another beer. He said, "Well, how was it?"

"What? Oh . . . that?" I shrugged. "It was fine."

He smiled for the second time that day with a look that said he knew more than I'd given him credit for. He didn't go to work, and after I was in bed that night, I heard him telling my mom the White Castle story. They both snickered, but I had no idea why. I get it now. They'd been sixteen once upon a time.

Jim was three months younger than I was, but Jack didn't allow him to apply for his license when he was sixteen. So for a few months I would take the car to Jim's occasionally after school. He wrote love letters to me in class during the day and gave me strict orders not to read them until I arrived back home. Once he poked around in my purse, supposedly looking for a pen. He called me that evening and told me to look in my powder compact. The little round applicator was missing, and in its place was a tiny note: *I wanted to give you an excuse to come by tomorrow.*

~*~

The following is one of the best:

10/19/64 2:15 p.m. "Joanna Lynn, I'm getting to miss you very much. I've thought of you all day. I miss you lover like I never have before. I remember your love for me and my love for you always. Oh, Joanna, I really do care and care so very much! To me, you're the nicest, sweetest girl I could ever know. I feel like everybody in the lab, in the whole school for that matter, should know I like you . . . I mean love you! All I can say is think about me and keep on loving me and we'll be happy and content. I got a book in the library about Automotive Fundamentals. I thought I'd better learn something about a car. Well, I'd better go, and I love you very much!

Jim. 2:30 p.m."

~*~

When Jim finally obtained his license, his dad helped him buy a car—a 1964 Yellow Rambler Classic. Jim moved twenty miles from Indianapolis to Greenfield, Indiana and rented a sleeping room from a mature Witness lady. With the assistance of an elder in the congregation, he started his own cleaning service. He opened a checking account at The Greenfield Banking Company under the name of J & J Janitorial & Carpet Cleaning Service. I thought the two "Js" stood for Jim and Joanna, but he informed me the other "J" was for his younger brother, Jerry. I assumed Jerry must've planned on moving to Greenfield after graduation. Jim cleaned a bank and car dealership at night. He signed up to be a Regular Pioneer, someone who spends a minimum of one-hundred hours every month in the ministry work.

Jim was proud of his Rambler and washed it every weekend, but it had a stick-shift and I'd never driven one. He decided he'd teach me. "It's easy, once you get the hang of it," he said, so we drove out into the middle of Hancock County where rural roads intersected at ninety-degree angles, but there was rarely any traffic. As it turned out, that was a good thing because I struggled with the concept of applying the clutch and brake in unison, rolling past stop signs by the dozens.

Dad liked Jim right away. Like Jim's dad, my dad was a machinist. This seemed to be the dominant theme of their conversations, and they'd spend time down in the basement in Dad's tool room for their manly talks. Dad showed Jim all of his old tools and explained what they were used for.

When Jim visited our house on weekends, Mom made chicken and dumplings from her grandmother's recipe, mashed potatoes with gravy, creamed peas and yeast rolls smothered with real butter. Her list of home-cooked meals was endless.

"Can you cook like your mother?" Jim said.

"Oh, Joanna makes dishes like you wouldn't believe," Dad chimed in before I could answer.

"I make a tuna casserole all the time," I said. "I love it!"

Jim frowned.

"You should taste her pies! She makes her own crust, you know," Mom said. "In fact, she made this butterscotch pie here, all except for the meringue. I made that myself. Joanna prefers whipped cream rather than meringue."

"Either are equally as good, though, you have to admit," Dad said, as he cut the pie into wedges.

Jim dug into a piece and was evidently convinced I was a good marriage candidate. The way to a man's heart . . . .

He proposed in the front seat of his 1964 yellow Rambler Classic. One evening I accompanied him to one of his Bible studies out in the county near Greenfield, and after he'd parked his car, he said, "Well here we are. But, wait . . . I want to ask you something."

I hadn't expected him to choose that moment to propose, even though we'd already agreed we wanted to be married. We'd browsed through a catalog of mail-order diamond engagement rings and I circled my favorite. How clever he was to slip my high school ring off my finger one evening and pretend to drop it. He claimed he didn't see it anywhere but he was sure it had rolled underneath the couch, at his parents' house. He said he'd retrieve it later. I knew he wanted to determine my finger size, so I played along. The next time we saw each other, he'd found my ring. Surprise!

Jim didn't want a traditional wedding. He claimed he'd feel self-conscious standing at the front of the Kingdom Hall, watching me walk up the aisle in a long gown. I was just fine with that. Even the thought of it made me feel faint. But I needed to check with my dad because Jim wanted us to walk up the aisle together. Would Dad feel slighted? I would have to ask him.

"You're marrying Jim, Princess, so he should have it however he wants. I won't feel left out." Dad laughed. "I'll be paying the bill for the reception. Having Jim as a son-in-law will be worth anything. He's a good man."

Our wedding took place on July 2, 1966 at the Brookside Kingdom Hall. On that anxious day, I gratefully breathed in the soothing, balsamic fragrance as I entered the reception area. The sweet, gingery soup smell of that place welcomed me in through the front door. JoAnn, my matron of honor and future sister-in-law, and I headed into the ladies room. I finished dressing and JoAnn secured my veil. I sent her out to see if Jim was there yet. He wasn't. What was keeping that guy? I knew he had a long list of errands to complete, but surely he wouldn't be late. It must have been the longest ten minutes of my life, waiting for him to arrive. A lot of the guests were there and seated. Finally, JoAnn burst through the restroom door and shouted, "He's here!" She'd turned "here" into a two-syllable word.

At precisely two o'clock in the afternoon, I walked toward my future husband, James Edward Coe, waiting for me right there in the foyer. Jim smiled lovingly and took my hand. Piano music beckoned from inside the auditorium, and as we began our walk together up the aisle, he whispered, "Here we go."

I'd said the same thing to Jehovah the day I was baptized.

~*~

36

Last summer at a writing workshop, I took a one-week course on sentencing. We were given an assignment to write one long sentence using the word "who" before each clause. This is what I wrote about Jim:

"He was the boy who caught my attention at the age of fifteen, who parted his hair way too far over on the right side, who was already a grown man at the age of fifteen, who was probably born an old man, who took on responsibilities generally reserved for older males, who carried the microphones at church meetings, who caught my eye over and over again, who wore thick glasses, who needed a girl to show him how to dress, who hated his father, who needed a wife, who proposed with a 1/10 ct. diamond engagement ring in the front seat of his yellow 1964 Rambler Classic, who walked hand and hand with me down the aisle to song number forty-three played on the piano, who accompanied me to the grocery on our wedding night and ate plums with me on the marital bed at the Holiday Inn, who finally understood his father, who became a father himself, who fathered my three sons, who loved his father, who became *my* father after my father died, who didn't like the way he was treated as an employee, who went into business determined to treat his employees better, who commandeered respect from his clients, who gained the attention of business associates, who became financially successful, who had zero turnover in his tool shop, who hired me as his bookkeeper, who paid me more than the job was worth."

~*~

"Here we go." He'd said it proudly—an eighteen-year old boy about to become a man. And if becoming a husband and losing one's virginity is a meter of manhood, he achieved both that day.

"Here we go." I've never forgotten those three spoken words and the tenderness with which he whispered them to me. He'd said it all—our adult lives were finally about to begin—as a couple.

Jim and I divorced twenty-three years later, and exactly four months from the day of our divorce he married his secretary. Nine years passed. Then, at the age of fifty, he was killed in a horrific tractor accident.

"Here we go."

Like a couple of kids at the top of the world's tallest rollercoaster, beginning our descent into one thriller of a ride.

Like we were supposed to be soul mates forever.

Like it was going to last an eternity.

I've thought often of that moment on the hottest July day in 1966, in the vestibule of the Brookside Kingdom Hall, the calming, familiar scent and those three words, and with that thought my throat closes up every time and my eyes tear. But I've never put those three words in *writing* like this. Until now. Now . . . my heart hurts, my wastebasket is full of damp tissues, and my laptop monitor is blurry. And only now do I appreciate that on that hot July day, Jim was already falling out of The Truth. He was way ahead of me.

CHAPTER FIFTEEN
HONEYMOON MADE IN WHERE?

Two eighteen-year old kids sped away from their wedding reception in a yellow Rambler, heading to a small, concrete block motel a few miles away. At that moment it could have led to honeymoon bliss or honeymoon disaster. Who knew? There they were, alone for the very first time and free to consummate their marriage with sexual intercourse. It was the moment they'd been waiting for. They'd bought a paperback sex manual and the groom had read it thoroughly. The bride breezed through it, deciding to wait and let her groom take care of the details. Surely he'd know what to do. It was against their religion to masturbate, so she had no idea how her body functioned. It would all come naturally though, of that she was confident. How difficult could it be, really?

~*~

The next day, they drove one-hundred miles in silence.

CHAPTER SIXTEEN
MARITAL BLISS WAS AN OXYMORON

Within a few days of our wedding, Jim's sixteen-year old brother moved in with us for some reason, although I was against it. Jim didn't give me a choice, and that right there changed our family dynamic. Jerry slept on the fold-out couch in the tiny living room at one end of our eight-foot wide trailer. Thirty-five feet away, right down the middle, through the kitchen with the pink appliances, through a miniature den, then the bath, was our bedroom. I can't describe it as having a central hallway because the rooms were separated only with sliding pocket doors. A three-quarter sized bed was squeezed in at the rear wall between two closets, his and hers, each no more than eighteen inches wide. I always suspected that Jerry could hear every little thing Jim and I said to one another, and I was sure he perked his ears up even more at the sound of our whispers.

We had no air-conditioning, which was not unusual for 1966. Sweaty love-making in a virtual oven didn't fit into *my* ideal marriage, and what had happened to the petting and making-out we'd done, even though we weren't supposed to? Foreplay in an oven would've been better than none at all. Our marriage got off to a pathetic start in a cramped hot-box.

Jim, being an ever practical, problem-solving kind of guy, went out and applied for a Sears Roebuck credit card, bought a 10,000 BTU air-conditioner and installed it in the rear window. Condensation methodically dripped onto the mattress below, on my side of the bed up against the wall. He proudly proclaimed that now I should have no excuse for not being sufficiently "turned on." The room was cool and the loud buzz from the window unit would drown out any sounds we'd make. But there was still the issue of privacy. The pocket doors opened freely with no locks. Our pink toilet was within two feet of our bedroom, and Jerry spent hours on it. I suspected he might slide the door a bit to peek through the crack.

CHAPTER SEVENTEEN
ONE MEAT, TWO VEGETABLES AND A SALAD

After my first few attempts at fixing our evening meals, Jim grumbled saying this was not the way supper was supposed to be. It should consist of one meat and two vegetables.

I tapped a fingernail on his Melamine plate. "Well, there's your fried pork chop next to a baked potato, and here's your lettuce salad."

"That's not two vegetables."

"What would you call it, then?"

"It's one vegetable and a salad. A green salad is not a vegetable—it's a salad," Jim said. "My mother could tell you that. Why can't you make mashed potatoes like hers?"

I picked up Jim's knife and fork and sliced the potato entirely into two halves. I put one half on either side of the pork chop. "There you go—two vegetables!"

"We've had baked potatoes three nights in a row." He threw both potato halves into the pink waste can, slammed out of the trailer and spun gravel as he rocketed his yellow Rambler out of its parking space. I could only imagine the neighbors, peeking through their glass louvers, knowing the newlyweds in the little pink trailer were at it again. (Yes, its exterior was pink, as well.)

The next day I emptied the trash and found a paper sack from Crider's Drive In. *Gosh darn it . . . he went out for a double Crider Burger and fries —my favorite!*

I made a phone call to his mother to inquire about her recipes, meals that Jim liked, but her "handful of this and a pinch of that" went way over my head. I needed specifics. I was only eighteen years old! She'd been cooking so long she didn't have anything more of substance to offer. I figured she could bake in her sleep if need be, so it's not like she was trying to make me suffer—she offered the best she could.

In tears, I called my mother. "How do you make mashed potatoes?"

She remained calm. "Didn't you receive three portable mixers at your reception?"

"Yes," I sobbed.

"Okay, then. Take one out of the box and store the other two—you've a lifetime of mixing ahead of you," she said. "Now write this down so you can refer back to it." She softly mentioned that she'd *tried* to teach me to cook while I was engaged, living at home. (I hadn't been the least bit interested. I mean, how hard could it be?)

"Don't remind me," I snapped.

"Call me tomorrow and let me know how it goes tonight," Mom said.

The only dish I excelled at was tuna casserole because I loved it so much, but Jim turned up his nose and wouldn't accept a casserole at all, not even tuna. Oh, yes, there was that exquisite pie crust Mom taught me to create, so I made Quiche Lorraine, but Jim didn't like his meat and vegetables mixed with eggs and cheese. Pie was pie, he said, and it was only for dessert, which comes *after* the meat, two vegetables and salad.

A few days later I went to Mom's house to do my laundry. A brand new Betty Crocker cookbook rested on our old kitchen table. She had inscribed on the inside: "For my daughter, the perfect housewife."

Oh, gag me, I thought. But I wore Betty Crocker out. And I made plenty more emergency phone calls to my mother for details. What's lemon zest? What does sauté mean? How do you cook spaghetti *al dente*? I hadn't even known that a simmer was a very low boil. Where had my head been, anyway? Finally, I perfected the art of the one meat/two vegetable/salad meal. Sometimes we had butterscotch or chocolate pie for dessert, with a homemade crust of course, topped with whipped cream.

Within no time Jim gained twenty, then thirty pounds, and I shied away from intimacy even more. What was the point, anyway? I'd been told to expect a fireworks finale, but we'd been married three months and I hadn't experienced anything but a few sparklers. According to the Organization, not only was masturbation a sin, but so was fantasizing and looking at pornography.

The excitement and stimulation I'd enjoyed while petting during courtship had come from knowing I was doing something I shouldn't. Since we were married, the proverbial carrot no longer dangled in front of me. Jim must have skipped the chapter in the sex manual about the importance of foreplay for the woman, and I remained ignorant enough not to experiment with my body because Jehovah was watching and would disapprove. In summary, the Organization's instructions on bedroom behavior, going even so far as which sexual positions and acts were acceptable to God, led me to feeling guilty for having normal human desires.

I asked Jim to go with me to see my Gynecologist. "Why should *I* go? You're the one who's frigid," he barked. I'd never thought of myself as frigid, and I was dismayed at his apathetic attitude, but I courageously made an appointment with my doctor and described my sexual dilemma. He shook his head. "Three months is nothing. Don't worry about that," he scolded. "Some women go three years before it happens." He waved me off. "Run along and relax—enjoy yourself."

Three years. *Three? He must be exaggerating*, I thought. Oh well. I shrugged, went home, feather-dusted the furniture and vacuumed the carpet. Then, I planned Jim's meals for the remainder of the week.

Jerry had finally moved out of our trailer in a huff, saying he couldn't stand the arguments. Jim and I couldn't go one week without a huge disagreement. I kept a diary with notations such as, "We haven't argued for six days!" or "It's been ten whole days since we quarreled!" Once I wrote it down, a major argument would usually ensue. We squabbled less after we had the trailer to ourselves, but not much.

The first difficult year of our marriage was coming to an end. As our anniversary approached, I entered an upscale luggage shop and put a hand-tooled Mexican-leather briefcase in the layaway for Jim. It excited me every Friday when I made a payment, thinking of how pleased he would be with the intricate design of it. That evening, I cooked a tender beef roast with mashed potatoes and gravy, green beans, a tossed salad and butterscotch pie for dessert. Jim brought me a syrupy sweet Hallmark card and a dozen red roses. When I gave him the briefcase, he frowned and said, "I can't carry this thing out in the ministry work."

"Why not?"

"It looks expensive. The householders' attention will be drawn to it and they'll think I'm materialistic."

I sighed and swallowed the lump in my throat. I'd bought a gift for Jim that I would've loved to have had for myself. "I guess I'll take it back to the store."

"No. I'll use it to store important papers. It's nice." He stuck it in the back of the closet.

The rose petals fell off day by day and the briefcase remained in the closet, not even venturing a trip to the Kingdom Hall. Jim was afraid of what the brothers and sisters would think of a bag so exquisite.

There was always something to disagree about and neither of us could hold our temper. We thought we knew exactly what the other should do. Or shouldn't do. After all, the Bible gave us instructions, enlarged upon by the Organization. The Rule Book was there. We weren't following the rules properly. Our expectations were unreasonably high, but neither of us saw that then. Jim, discouraged by his failure as head of the house, gave up trying. I respected him even less for giving up.

I have since removed the word "should" from my vocabulary.

Wouldn't I love to go back and do it all again, knowing what I know now? Yet, who hasn't wished for such a thing? Regrets, we all have them, I suppose, and those are mine.

CHAPTER EIGHTEEN
BRAINWASHING OR PERSUASION?

By definition, brainwashing is "the application of coercive techniques to change the values and beliefs, perceptions and judgments, and subsequent mindsets and behaviors of one or more people, usually for political, financial, personal, or religious purposes."

The vast majority of ex-Witnesses believe the Organization is a cult which uses brainwashing techniques. For those who feel so strongly, that may be true for them. And while I might have been a good candidate for brainwashing, that term is not an accurate one I'd use for my own experience. *Persuasion* is more precise. At least, that's what I choose to believe.

For example: Have you ever been approached by someone while walking past a kiosk at a shopping mall? "Madam? If you wouldn't mind . . ." he said. The attractive dark-eyed man wasn't from here, I could tell. More likely from Europe, or perhaps the Middle East, somewhere exotic that I'd never been but had always wanted to visit. I caught the scent of Bvlgari. Nice. He continued without hesitation, "I'd like your opinion on this brand new product—nothing in the world like it, until now. Oprah featured it on her show just last week. Did you see it? No?" He reached for my hand. "You'll be amazed to see what this can do for you." Oh, he was smooth! I didn't want to take the time, but he smelled delicious and I couldn't walk away from him. He had me at "Madam" even though I knew he only wanted to sell me something I didn't need and couldn't afford. But, Oprah? Well, if *she* says this product will assure you of everlasting life in the remake of the Garden of Eden, I'll take a closer look. This guy put me in the mind of a professional snake oil salesman! He massaged both of my hands with cleansers, tonics, cuticle creams, revitalizing oils and a mud mask, describing each in detail, never leaving a breath of space for me to object. "And guess what!" He pointed toward Nordstrom's at the end of the mall. "*They* don't sell this product. Only here." He grinned. He sure was handsome. "Only me . . . today!" *Wow*, I thought, *this is my lucky day*. I handed him my American Express card and walked away with a shopping bag full of goodies. What I'd wanted the most was the royal blue porcelain container of mud mask that

Oprah loves; her skin was so smooth and healthy. But, it could not be purchased alone. No? No. It could only be obtained (at a special price of only fifty dollars) if you bought the entire line of other useless junk. By the time I reached the parking lot, I wondered if other shoppers could see the word *gullible* scribbled across my forehead.

That was four years ago. The blue flying saucer-shaped porcelain container looks spectacular on my dressing table. I've used the mud mask only three times, but my skin is healthier by osmosis, by having the container so close to all my other cosmetics. Maybe I should rethink the brainwashing idea. *The application of coercive techniques to change the beliefs and subsequent mindsets of someone for financial purposes?* I was brainwashed in fifteen minutes time at the Oxmoor Mall in Louisville, Kentucky!

When I visit the mall, I see the kiosk and the familiar attractive salesman with a potential buyer's hands slathered with lotions and potions. I make it a point to walk on the opposite side of the aisle. He'd said, "Only here, only me, today," and had swayed me to make my decision immediately. It couldn't wait. *He* couldn't wait—hurry now—he had other shoppers to influence, to *persuade*. I was the perfect candidate.

~*~

At each Circuit and District Assembly, presentations depicted what acceptable family life looked like according to the Bible. Typical settings for these dramas began with a folding card table and four chairs, a father, mother and two loving, obedient children—the model family. The father picked up the Bible, or the Daily Text Book, or any number of other Watchtower publications and announced that it was time for the family Bible study. The children trotted over to the table with glee and took their seats. Wifey removed her apron, laid her feather duster down and sat next to her husband. He offered a prayer, and the wife and children—in submission to the father as the spiritual head of the household—followed his lead by enthusiastically participating in the family Bible study.

I couldn't help but be reminded of the Dick Van Dyke Show in the sixties, or Father Knows Best in the early fifties. Rob Petrie, in his business suit, walks through the front door after work and his wife Laura, with her apron on, is waiting for hubby with a plastic smile on her pretty face. More often than not they sit down to a homemade meal prepared by the wife, and if little Ritchie, or Bud, Betty or Kitten needed discipline, guess whose job that was? Rob Petrie or Jim Anderson. The man was in charge of his family, or so it appeared.

It was our understanding, as we watched the current-day vaudeville displays on stage at assemblies, that we should follow these God-given examples to create our family life exactly as had been shown to us. These dramatizations *persuaded* me to believe it was entirely possible to have a peaceful and productive weekly family Bible study.

I do give Jim credit for at least trying these techniques—he tried to be the spiritual leader of our two-person family, but we were both used to studying our Watchtower lessons by ourselves. We were two stubborn and independent individuals. Whenever he tried to study a chapter of a book with me, possibly for an upcoming meeting, he never did it properly and I told him so.

"If I'm going to be in submission to you, then you need to conduct our study in a correct manner." In Jim's defense, and as you can see, I was not an easy wife to tame. I knew it all—I was an only child. I'll say no more about that because if you've ever known one, you'll know exactly what I'm talking about. Jim, fond of attaching labels to people, eventually diagnosed me: The Only Child Syndrome. I blush even now as I write about it.

PART TWO

CHAPTER NINETEEN
MY (PARENTHETICAL) PHASE

"In the end, I believe appreciation is of much more value than worship." ~ from Chapter Fifty-Three

If I live to be ninety, half of my life will have been frittered away within parenthetical brackets. Forty-five years as a Jehovah's Witness placed me in the middle of the world of humankind, but I was not allowed to be a vital part of it, making me a phrase, clause or sentence (within a parenthesis). I consider those chapters of my life my parenthetical *phase.*

While I might have subtly interrupted the syntactic construction of a paragraph, I did not affect it. Highly discouraged from having opinions (let alone expressing them) about the world around me, I had plenty to say, but no one heard me because I did not allow myself the luxury of speaking my mind.

So far, the majority of this story was written from the perspective of what I believed during the forty-five years I was in The Truth—one of Jehovah's Witnesses, when I had no doubt that Jehovah God, though invisible, was *not* imaginary. I developed a heartfelt love for Jehovah and considered Him to be a true friend. I believed that He created everything, so I prayed to Him, relied on Him and worshipped Him. Now, after the passing of many years and trials, I wonder if He was actually real. Or was He a figment of my imagination? He certainly *felt* real during the time of my religious belief, but I carried faith, belief and imagination in one basket. That's how it is with faith—the way it *has* to be, really.

"Faith is the *assured expectation of things hoped for*, the evident demonstration of realities though not beheld." Hebrews 11:1 (New World Translation) In other words: What one believes to be true has power over them, yet what one believes is often based on mere perception. One dictionary definition of "believe" is "to have confidence in the truth, the existence, or the reliability of something, although without *absolute proof* that one is right in doing so." And the following example is given in one sentence: "Only if one *believes* in something can one act purposefully."

So, what *can* we believe? If we base our life's purpose on our beliefs, I've reached one simple conclusion—we ought to believe anything we choose. Why not? Most people follow that practice even though they might not realize it. I chose to believe in God. He was intangible, an imaginary friend, but my faith in Him suited my purpose for over four decades.

Most days, I don't believe there is a god anymore. Occasionally, I think maybe there is, but for me, He or She or It is *not* a god who knows our every thought (or even *cares* what we're thinking), who will strike a match and torture us forever if we refuse to follow specific, complicated and oftentimes silly rules. When I hold a newborn, I believe there *must* be a god. When I see violent anger and hate among the human race, I figure there *cannot* be a god. I walk outside on a spring day—birds sing and a fresh breeze ruffles my hair—or I witness a glorious sunrise; then I think *maybe* there is a god. But when I see the insensitive, unnecessary bickering and wars between peoples of various religions, I truly believe with all of my heart that if a god exists, he is involved in the self-serving beliefs of these people only in their imaginations. I confess I want to believe in God, first of all because I followed that comfortable path for nearly half a century; second, I like the *feeling* of having a Higher Power watching over me.

I've studied both sides now, Creation and Evolution, God or No God. Neither theory has been proven to my satisfaction. I look to the sky and I see clouds . . . or teddy bears, or dragons, or a face . . . each design a perception of my imagination. On clear days there are no clouds visible, no evidence of God if one believes a god created clouds. Yet, clouds are scientifically explained, which, for me, argues against a god creation.

I often call to mind the songwriter Joni Mitchell's words. She looked at clouds from up and down but only recalled clouds' illusions. She didn't really *know* clouds at all.

The common phrase "Don't Lose the Faith" has been popular for decades. Did I *lose* faith? No, I merely gave up my need for the assured expectation of things hoped for, my need to know for a certainty. I didn't lose my faith, but I changed what I put my faith in. On any given day, my imagination allows me to experience the joy of living without the benefit of knowing. What I believe to be true on Monday might not be what I choose to believe on Tuesday. When I got untethered from the comfort of religion, it wasn't a loss of faith for me, it was a discovery of self.

Bill Maher, the politically incorrect stand-up comedian, says he doesn't believe in religion, or in god, but he believes in love. I believe in love, too. I've always believed in its power and I always will. That is one thing I've never had doubts about, but I no longer feel the need for religion at all, although I appreciate that many people do. Let them believe whatever they want. Let the Atheists and Creationists argue about evolution vs. creation until they are blue in the face, if they wish. I have no interest in arguing about this issue. In fact, it is not an issue for me.

The rear of my vehicle isn't decorated with a cross in the center of a fish. If I had one, my bumper sticker would read: Ambivalent Non-Believer.

I stayed with my religious belief-system for so long because I loved our Heavenly Creator, wholehearted in my belief that it was the only true religion. I still love Him, too, although on the days when I tend not to believe, it's the *memory* of Jehovah I love. He saw me through some rough times and for that, I'm grateful.

~*~

Eventually dissatisfied with my uncertainty and doubts about Jehovah's Witness doctrine, I prayed for direction. Over and over, repeatedly I prayed. My prayer was answered in a most unusual way, an answer that left no doubt in my mind.

A few of my friends and family were stunned when I discarded organized religion, but an attack on my dignity opened the doorway for my exit. In reality, that door had always been open, but I didn't see it because of the blinders I'd been wearing. I needed a good old-fashioned nudge over the edge. That's what I got, and I believed at the time it came from God.

Jehovah's Witnesses would tell you otherwise, but this is *my* story.

CHAPTER TWENTY
MOVING ON DOWN THE ROAD

"Ring the bells that still can ring, forget your perfect offering. There is a crack, a crack in everything. That's how the light gets in." ~ Leonard Cohen

The United States deployed combat units to Vietnam in 1965. The Selective Service draft lottery was in effect, and the JW brothers who did not qualify for a draft-exempt 4D Minister's Classification were sentenced to prison for the two or three years they would've ordinarily served their country. The Watchtower Society exalted these brothers, comparing them to Job who was tempted and punished by Satan for not renouncing his loyalty to God. But they were labeled as cowards by the rest of the world, and the Organization's self-appointed heroic status didn't impress fellow inmates at the prisons where these brothers were incarcerated.

A 4D was obtainable either by serving in some capacity at Bethel, the Organization's headquarters in Brooklyn, New York, or by spending a minimum of 100 hours per month in the door-to-door ministry work—a regular pioneer. Jim had no interest in going away to Bethel, so his only route to a 4D was to pioneer. Jim signed up the week after he graduated from high school and moved to Greenfield. While I'd known this would prevent him from being drafted when he turned nineteen, I also believed he genuinely *wanted* to pioneer.

Like I said, Jim was falling out of The Truth even before I was and it was this draft-avoidance issue that triggered it. After the war ended, he admitted that he had never been wholehearted about pioneering, he'd spent numerous hours alone in the ministry work, knocking on one or two doors, then napped in the car the remainder of the afternoon. Jim knew his real motives and waged a battle with his nagging conscience because of the dishonesty, but he couldn't see himself facing the Draft Board without a 4D. He could not enlist as a CO (conscientious objector) because the Organization did not allow it—Jehovah was going to bring Armageddon to Earth—a war He would battle with all nations of the world. Jehovah would be the supreme victor. For us to join any army now would label us as traitors, serving in the camp of the enemy. Our allegiance was only to Jehovah via his

Organization. For that reason, we did not stand for the National Anthem, salute the flag or cast our vote in elections. We were to remain neutral in all affairs of the world. Jehovah's Witnesses didn't celebrate national holidays, nor were we patriotic in any way. *Neutrality* was our staunch position. My schoolmates had been unmerciful in the '50's, called me a traitor and the dirtiest word of all—a Communist!

I worried about Jim's unhappiness. I thought it was due to our troubled marriage but later comprehended the much larger concern. After one year of marriage, we moved our pink trailer to a park in Indianapolis, one mile down the road from The Indianapolis Speedway. We heard the roar of Indy cars racing at record speeds on Memorial Day each year. Jim decided to become a machinist and work for his father who would teach him the trade. I billed patients and transcribed office reports full-time for a Urologist in downtown Indianapolis in the building where my mother worked as a secretary for a General Surgeon.

Jim developed a habit of attending all of the weekly meetings for a month or two, then he'd slack off, claim to be working late or not feeling well, and within a few weeks he stopped attending altogether. I detested going to the meetings alone because everyone would ask where my husband was. I made up creative excuses, never admitting, not even to myself, that he was spiritually sick. The elders questioned me repeatedly about Jim. I was in a *man's club*—they weren't the least bit interested in my spiritual well-being —only Jim's. It was the husband's place to assist his wife to advance her spirituality. When the elders showed up at our door, Jim would not answer and ordered me not to, either. I felt like a typical householder hiding from a door-to-door magazine salesman. One persistent brother cornered me before a Sunday meeting and said he'd visited the day before but Jim pretended he wasn't at home.

I frowned. "Jim wouldn't do that. Maybe he was taking a shower, or perhaps he was asleep. When was it?"

The brother replied, "Yesterday, and no he wasn't sleeping. I made sure of it! I beat on the front door, the back door and all of the windows."

I put on a surprised expression. *Hmmm*, I thought. So *he's* the big, bad wolf who'd tried to blow our house down. I couldn't let on that I'd been there the entire time. I shook my head and lied with a straight face. "I can assure you, he wasn't at home if he didn't answer."

"His car was there," he hissed, his face contorted like an ugly rattlesnake about to strike.

I shrugged. "We like to take walks through the trailer park."

The brother grunted and walked away—left me standing completely alone.

We moved time and again, from one congregation to another, but the routine started all over again in a new congregation. Our pink home on wheels logged more miles than an eighteen-wheeler.

CHAPTER TWENTY-ONE
DIARY IN A CORNFIELD

We'd been married two years when a Circuit Overseer talked to Jim about his spiritually weakened condition. The overseer suggested we move far away and start over. He proposed we travel to serve as pioneers where the need was great. Lewisburg, Tennessee had only nine adult members in their congregation with two counties to cover, so they desperately needed more warm bodies. Jim planned to boost his spirituality and I figured it would work wonders for mine, as well. At that time, I hadn't heard the wise saying, "Wherever you go, there you are."

On October 28, 1968, after my dad helped Jim pack our personal belongings into a little utility trailer we were to pull behind our car, Mom stood at the curb in front of their house and took our picture as we waved goodbye. I tried to ignore the tears forming in her eyes. She told me later she'd fallen into my dad's arms and bawled after we drove away.

Interstate-65 was still under construction, so we worked our way slowly through city traffic without a problem until we picked up the expressway south of Indianapolis. Within five minutes after reaching 65 MPH, we felt a thump and heard a whooshing sound. I jerked around, peering out the rear window in time to see our most precious possessions flying all over the highway and into the adjacent cornfield. The utility trailer appeared empty. Automobiles honked and swerved to avoid boxes, clothes and broken items. We veered to the shoulder and haphazardly dodged cars as we ran on and off the highway after each vehicle whizzed by, collecting whatever we could salvage. Jim cussed and mumbled as we foraged through the cornfield, blaming the poor packing job on my dad who, even though he'd been drinking the night before, assured Jim everything was securely fastened. I blew the corn silks and dirt off my Betty Crocker cookbook, a prized Nancy Drew book, bank statements and an empty manila envelope labeled *1967 Taxes*, all the while shaking my head in disbelief at our misfortune. Satisfied we'd found everything of value, we repacked the trailer with the help of a motorist who'd stopped to assist us.

Jim and I knew nothing about Daylight Savings Time. We'd never changed our clocks and hadn't traveled enough to know anyone else did. Sunday morning, we pulled into the gravel parking lot of a little building which sufficed as the Lewisburg Kingdom Hall. We had overslept, rushed to arrive on time, and were baffled as to why no one else was there. Jim recalled hearing something about a time change and he figured that's where we'd gone wrong. I'd never heard of such a strange practice, but we had an extra hour to study our *Watchtower* magazine, since we hadn't done it already. I was proud—I'd be in the audience with all of my answers underlined!

The first car to arrive was Brother Adcox, the Congregation Overseer. He'd been delighted to welcome us to his congregation when we'd met him the previous month while making our plans to move. But a new development brought a conflict. Brother Zander and his wife and six children had moved down from Pennsylvania, allegedly to give the tiny congregation some assistance. Zander was a smooth, fast talker and had impressed Adcox with multi-syllable words and compliments. However, behind Adcox's back, Zander made fun of the elderly man and everything about the backwards little Tennessee town. I thought if he loved the North so much he should've stayed there.

Adcox had lived in middle Tennessee all of his life, and he spoke with the typical southern drawl. Shelbyville was a town close to Lewisburg, and we had gone together one Saturday to cover the rural territory there. When Adcox got out of the car, Zander made a snide remark about being in "Shovel" which is exactly what it sounded like when Adcox said it.

It seemed a competition had begun between Jim and Zander as to who could help the Lewisburg Congregation the most before we actually set down roots. Adcox had a way of teasing Jim, bragging constantly about Zander's maturity, his experience and his aggressiveness. Jim withered with frustration and was made to feel inferior. Although I naively thought it was all done in jest, Jim had a different viewpoint. He took it personally.

Adcox pulled into the parking lot that Sunday morning, rolled down his window and guffawed, "You got here an hour early, didn't you? I knew you would. Hah! Wait till I tell Brother Zander!"

Jim looked at me with puppy dog eyes and said, "If he only knew Zander calls him a country bumpkin."

"Don't say anything," I said. "Leave it up to Jehovah to handle Zander." A mainstay of the Organization's teachings was that any seeming injustices would eventually be handled by Almighty God, and to attempt to take matters into one's own hands would show a lack of faith in Jehovah's abilities to execute discipline or vengeance.

Jim heaved a sigh as he exited the car and slammed his door.

Adcox introduced us to a few people at the meeting, and he always inserted the juicy news that we'd arrived an hour early because we hadn't a clue about Daylight Savings Time. Ha, ha.

Jim pounded his fist on the steering wheel on the way home from the meeting. "This place is ridiculous. We might as well pack up and move."

"We just made it down here," I cried.

"Yeah. Well I wish we hadn't. I don't have a good feeling about this."

"Try to ignore those immature morons, okay? It's not about them—it's about helping the people down here. We can do that."

Jim promised to give it a chance. "But, I suspect Zander is running from something," he said. "Take one look at him and you can tell, can't you? Look at his slicked-back hair and the way he swaggers around like he's big man on campus. That kind of attitude probably got him kicked out of Pittsburg; I'd bet money on it."

I weighed his words and intuitively knew he was right. There most definitely was a secret in that awful man's past—I could feel it just like in the soap operas I'd become addicted to. I often wondered what his wife saw in her husband, and why she allowed a man to dominate her the way he did.

I searched for my diary that night to journal the account of the dreadful trip and the ghastly start we'd made. My diary was missing—*all* of my diaries were missing! I'd been keeping one each year since I was fifteen and had kept them carefully packed in a small box. I couldn't hold back my tears as it occurred to me that my precious words, thoughts delicately formed into sentences and paragraphs, had undoubtedly been left behind in that Indiana cornfield, perhaps stuck to the giant wheel of a semi-truck, going round and round, just like my life. My diaries were a large part of *me* and now they were lost forever. I was embarrassed because a Hoosier farmer might stumble across my journals and find out how many days we had between arguments during our first year of marriage. What if a trucker had retrieved my intimate notes about our first kiss on Jim's front porch? Or, even worse, what about the times I'd written about Jim and I making out like crazy. I was ashamed of doing it (I hadn't recognized it as a natural way for an engaged couple to behave), so I'd recorded it and gone on to feel embarrassed for even writing it down! What if a greasy trucker found those pages and recited them to a bunch of drunken fools for their amusement at a truck stop bar? At least I'd never journaled about my inability to have an orgasm. I couldn't even admit that to myself, especially not on paper. I no longer had a good feeling about this move either.

~*~

I made telephone sales calls part-time at the local Sears Catalogue store. Jim claimed to work part-time in a tool shop in Nashville. In reality, he worked forty hours per week, putting money away for the time we would move yet again. However, he reported to the congregation on his publisher's time slip over 100 hours of field service every month, which would have been possible only if he were witnessing to his coworkers all the live-long day. On Saturday mornings, while I prepared for field service, he stayed in bed, saying he already had his time in during the week.

I wonder if he ever actually witnessed to anyone?

CHAPTER TWENTY-TWO
THE TWENTY-ONE GUN SALUTE

During the next seven months, I rarely managed to meet my quota of required field-service time because of my discouragement regarding Jim's low spiritual level—the supposed spiritual head of the house. There we were, in a new location with new friends, but *we* were the same as before. While we managed to tolerate old Brother Adcox and holier-than-thou Zander, we really didn't like *us*.

One evening in mid-May 1969, I was invited to accompany a pioneer sister on a Bible study in the adjoining county. I figured it would give me a break, time away from Jim and a couple easy hours' service to report, so I agreed. She pulled into our gravel driveway later that night, and Jim flipped on the porch light and stood at the door, waiting. I knew something was wrong. He asked me to sit down.

"Your dad died," he said. "Your mom found him on the bathroom floor when she came home from work. It was a heart attack."

Unbelievable—he was only fifty-one! *Of course it was a heart attack*, I thought. He'd had one four years earlier while I was in high school. In those days there was very little to do for heart disease surgically. He'd been instructed to rest, eat healthy and give up cigarettes and alcohol, but he continued to drink and smoke as before. His addictions had done him in. I imagined his heart thought, *if you're not going to take care of me—I quit!*

We tossed our clothes into a suitcase and drove six hours to Indianapolis, arriving early the next morning. Mom and I hugged and cried, and cried some more. Dad hadn't felt well that morning, but Mom had assumed he was hung-over and she left for work. She'd called home, but never received an answer.

The police said he passed away suddenly, very early in the day, probably shortly after she'd left the house. They assured her there would have been nothing she could have done for him. Still, she thought if she'd stayed home maybe she could've called an ambulance and he might have been revived. It was another six months before she felt comfortable being left alone in that house.

Mom bought an expensive coffin and a completely unnecessary concrete vault, but she refused to purchase the suit they suggested as he still had the one he'd worn one time, three years before at my wedding. The funeral director explained since Dad had served in the United States Navy during World War II, an American flag would drape his coffin. I wondered what the congregation members would think when they saw it. We wouldn't salute the flag, and yet my father's coffin was to be covered with one. During the visitation, I heard Mom explaining to several people that it was because of his military service. Everyone compassionately nodded, and I was less apprehensive.

Mom's congregation overseer, Brother Hayes, delivered the funeral talk. I respected Brother Hayes for his kindness and sincerity. He spoke knowledgeably of my father, had known him personally, and had been the only Jehovah's Witness Dad liked, of the several who'd tried for years to convert my father.

There was just no hope for my dad's future, I thought. He'd not joined in The Truth, he'd smoked and drank profusely and blurted out the occasional cuss word. At the cemetery, I took Brother Hayes aside. "Do you think my dad will be in Paradise?"

He promptly grasped my hand. "Well, of course he'll be resurrected. Jehovah will give him a second chance—have no doubt."

What a relief! If Brother Hayes believed it, then it was good enough for me. There I was, at the age of twenty-one, still relying on opinions of other folks rather than thinking for myself.

Several military personnel stood at attention, and finally, when his coffin was about to be lowered, they raised their rifles to give my father the twenty-one gun salute. I cringed, wondering what our JW comforters and friends were thinking.

When Mom was ceremoniously handed the flag folded into a triangle, she promptly asked my Uncle Howard if he'd like to have it. Howard considered it an honor. He'd also served in the Navy with my dad during WWII.

Visitors stopped by throughout the next few days. Oddly enough, each one brought a meatloaf. Not a casserole or cake in sight. After eating meatloaf for a week, we stored what was left in Mom's freezer. Jim and I stayed with my mother for several weeks since she couldn't tolerate being at home alone. Six weeks had gone by when a small box arrived addressed to Charles Foreman. Curious, Mom opened it, only to find a set of four individual pizza pans. Mom knew Dad had ordered them, but she'd forgotten all about it. We both felt Dad had stopped by for a visit. We had ourselves a good cry which turned into laughter. We opened the Betty Crocker cookbook to find a pizza crust recipe, and we tried all sorts of toppings. We thanked Dad for the new pizza pans as we wrapped each individual pizza securely, storing them in the freezer for quick snacks later on. We threw out the remaining freezer-burned rectangles of meatloaf. I never cared for meatloaf in the first place, and to this day I can't stand it. I store Dad's pizza pans with my cake and pie plates in my own kitchen now.

~*~

Charles Leroy Foreman was born on Christmas Day, which I thought truly amazing, before I learned Jesus wasn't actually born on that day. I wondered how many other people could brag about that honor, sharing a birthday with Jesus!

Dad was a tool and die maker by trade and had worked for a variety of machine shops, the latest being the Chrysler plant in Indianapolis. When he wasn't sporting a crew cut, his hair was slicked back with Brylcreem (a little dab'll do ya), lending to the appearance of a "retro" model you'd see in one of today's fashion magazines. His daily "uniform" was a pleated pair of cuffed dress pants and a white sleeveless undershirt. When he wore a shirt, it was long-sleeved, and he liked to roll the cuffs up to right below the elbow. He relaxed around the house in his stocking feet (black socks, never white) and left for work in leather casual loafers, although I assumed he stored his work boots at the shop. I never saw him in flip-flops, although back then we called them thongs. In any case, he didn't like anything between his toes, with the exception of warm sand. He could spend an entire afternoon on the narrow, sandy beach beside Brandywine Creek with an iced-down six-pack or two.

Dad had a favorite chair in the living room and he occupied the same seat each day at the kitchen table. It was at that table I learned about "spuds."

"Pass the spuds," he'd say, and while Mom often served the creamiest mashed potatoes ever to melt in our mouths, spuds equally applied to the baked and fried variety. Whenever I see or hear the word "spud" I remember my dad and the happy family times we had. He was agreeable and good-natured, argumentative only when he'd been drinking heavily. He had a tendency to be silly when intoxicated, so every day with him was a new adventure. One night he went down on all fours and pretended to eat from the dog's bowl. I ignored him, walked out of the room and turned off the kitchen light, leaving him entirely alone. Now I wish I'd laughed, or said something. *Anything.* He merely wanted to entertain me, or perhaps he needed some attention. Who's to say?

He was an alcoholic, although we didn't label him as such. He simply had a *drinking problem*, emblematic of the elephant in the room everyone walks around and doesn't speak of. A few weeks before he died, he said to my mother, "What the hell do you suppose is wrong with me?" Mom and I talked about this often during the days after the funeral. We figured if he hadn't died so young, he might have eventually found sobriety through Alcoholics Anonymous.

Dad's chair was a swivel rocker, Deco style, upholstered in brown tweed on the seat and back, and half way down the arms. The remainder of the arms and splayed legs were made of beautifully polished maple wood. One day when I was still very little, after he'd been drinking all afternoon and had fallen asleep in his chair, I nudged the chair around a few degrees, enough to station myself behind him with a comb and some rubber bands. I gave him two of the cutest tiny pony tails you've ever seen on a man. I washed the oily hair cream off my hands and wandered off with Dainy into another room to play. An hour or so later, when Dad woke up, he laughed and called to me, asking me to re-do his style. As hard as I tried, the little "horn" shapes would not lie down, and he went through the remainder of the week with two obvious lumps on the top of his head.

During visitation at the funeral home, a co-worker of Dad's introduced himself. He informed me of my father's weekly ritual—flipping his wallet open and saying, "Have you seen a picture of my little princess?" The man recalled the days when Dad proudly walked through the shop, patting those two little bumps in his hair, saying his little girl was just as cute as a button, wasn't she?

CHAPTER TWENTY-THREE
BACK HOME AGAIN IN INDIANA

Jim used Dad's death to justify our move back home to Indiana, away from Lewisburg where the elders suspected he wasn't what he claimed to be. I was happy to live close to my mother once again. The next year, Mom sold our house, bought a mobile home and signed up to pioneer. Jim and I attended a new congregation in Lizton, a few miles west of Indianapolis. Jim claimed, somewhere along the line, his hand-tooled leather briefcase had been stolen from the trunk of our car. That case held our Publisher Record Cards, and he was afraid for anyone to see his record of monthly service; he did not want anyone in Lizton to be aware that he had moved around so much. While packing many years later for yet another move, I found the briefcase, not stolen at all, and only then did I get the bigger picture of what Jim had been doing, or not doing.

Once the Lizton elders began to close in on Jim, he decided it would be best to move farther away. The draft had ended, and Jim didn't intend to continue pioneering, nor did he plan to remain in The Truth. He no longer wanted to live a hypocritical life, but he didn't share those motives or plans with me at the time. If he'd have told me what was on his mind, I could've absorbed it and carried on. I didn't comprehend that Jim was no longer interested on keeping up a façade because I hadn't realized it was one.

He chose Louisville as our next destination, just far enough away from Indianapolis so his family wouldn't know he'd slacked off and quit. I once again called the mobile home movers, packed my breakables, and taped the kitchen cabinets shut for the one-hundred mile journey.

We'd lived in Louisville for two years when I became pregnant with our first son, Jesse. We sold the little trailer and moved into a townhouse apartment, causing us to cross a boundary line and make a Kingdom Hall change. I felt it from the beginning—the Woodlawn Congregation of Jehovah's Witness was made up of genuinely happy people. I was much more at home at Woodlawn than anywhere else since our marriage. Jim attended an occasional meeting but never went in the ministry work. Still, we were moderately content during that period of our lives. Not only were we excited to have a child, but I met Emma, who eventually became my dearest friend of all time. She was real. I did not imagine her. She was nine years old when I began attending the Woodlawn Congregation. I was twenty-five and she was curious about my pregnancy and followed me all over the Kingdom Hall before and after our five meetings each week. I couldn't shake that kid! I happily became Emma's mentor. Rather than hinder our relationship, the sixteen year difference in our ages added to the uniqueness of it.

CHAPTER TWENTY-FOUR

MY BEST FRIEND EMMA

1992—Emma stared at a spot on the ceiling so intensely she didn't notice when I walked into the room and took a seat adjacent to her bed. I reached for her hand, the one without the I.V., and I gave it a little squeeze.

She looked at me with those enchanting emerald eyes of hers, not attempting to mask her fear. "What if it's cancer?" she whimpered.

"It won't be," I said quickly with a reassuring smile. It *can't* be, I thought.

Her sun-bleached hair lay undisturbed on the starched white pillow without a trace of having been in emergency surgery for three hours. The surgeon had removed a large ovarian mass—a tumor he called it. Fortunately, Emma had lost very little blood; Jehovah's Witnesses were not allowed to accept blood transfusions, not even to save a life.

I ran my fingers carefully through her blonde curls as I studied her pale face.

The corners of her mouth formed a pout. "It was the size of a cantaloupe," she sniffed.

I shook my head in a most authoritative manner. "Something that large is merely a cyst. Cancer is never that big, honey."

She thought for a minute. "They say it doesn't look good."

"Well, of course it didn't." I sighed. "What cantaloupe-sized cyst would look *good* for heaven's sakes?"

"Not that kind of good, you goofball!" Emma laughed. "Ouch!" She placed one hand on her abdomen. "It hurts when I laugh."

"Then, don't!" I laughed along with her and after awhile I added, "Everything is going to be fine. Try not to worry about it."

Emma was twenty-eight years old and had everything in the world to look forward to: two young sons, Anthony and Joey, and her husband Thomas who'd adored her since the day they met as teenagers. Plus, she had me, her best friend. She *couldn't* have cancer! She would not, I decided.

~*~

During the course of Emma's surgery, an entourage of Witnesses had assembled in the main waiting room at Jewish Hospital in downtown

Louisville. Most of them were members of the Woodlawn Congregation where Emma and I had begun our friendship so long ago. Jim and I and our children had moved across the Ohio River to a small Hoosier town and hadn't seen some of these dear friends for awhile. I was happy to sit and chat with them and catch up while we waited. No one had to ask, "What are *you* doing on this side of the river?" Elders, family, and congregation members were all aware of the close relationship Emma and I had shared throughout the years.

After Emma regained consciousness, Thomas told her I was downstairs with the others, and I was the only one she asked for. She instructed him to tell the nurse I was her sister so they'd let me into the ICU. She'd wanted me by her side at that life-threatening moment and that's right where I belonged.

Emma and I chatted for a few minutes more, and after we agreed to thoroughly discount the doctor's suggestion of cancer in the ugly cantaloupe-shaped cyst, we planned a trip to our favorite Mexican restaurant for margaritas as soon as she was released from the hospital.

A nurse needed to examine Emma's dressing and perform other post-surgical tasks, so I followed the hallway to a small waiting lounge. Thomas was sprawled on the couch while Emma's parents had taken their sons to the cafeteria. Thomas opened his eyes and said, "What do you think?"

I shrugged one shoulder. "She's tough; she'll be fine."

"You think so?" He was not optimistic.

I sat in the chair next to him and patted his shoulder. "Try not to worry about her. I can't believe it's as serious as they're trying to make out."

He shook his head and stared at the floor. "Seems there's a history of ovarian cancer in her family."

"Oh." That's all I could say. I shuddered; someone from up above had poured a bucket of ice water on me. Still, I figured she was too young to worry about it and I wanted to steer Thomas's mind toward a happier place. "I remember the first time I saw Emma," I said. "It was before you ever knew her, back in the spring of '73."

That brought a smile to his face. "Seriously?"

"Sure thing. I was twenty-five, pregnant with Jesse, and going door-to-door."

"Emma was . . . what . . . nine?" Thomas asked. "I knew you two went a long way back."

I nodded. We sat quietly for a few minutes.

Emma's family drifted into the room. Emma's father threw his arms around me and squeezed tighter than ever before. "Hey *JoEmma*! I knew you'd be here." Every Sunday after the meeting, we'd walked across the street to the grill at the Woodlawn Bowling Alley for lunch. Her dad had designated the nickname for me in the grill one day after he noticed his daughter and I were so much alike that we routinely finished one another's sentences.

The nurse peeked in and invited everyone back to the patient's room. Lydia, Emma's mother, was also a close friend. She reached for me, requesting me to follow, but I declined. I didn't want to horn in on their time together, today of all days. I told her I'd come back tomorrow. "Call me if there's any new information," I said as they trailed out of the waiting room.

~*~

On the drive home, my thoughts were of my best friend. That day way back in 1973, we had met at the Kingdom Hall with others from our congregation, preparing to go door-to-door. As the elder arranged our car groups, Emma raised her hand for permission to speak. "I'd like to work with Joanna today!" She asked permission to touch my protruding abdomen and said, "I'm going to have children someday." I told her I thought she'd be a fine mother, having no idea that we would share a pregnancy and baby experience less than ten years later.

The car group reached its assigned territory where Emma and I were dropped off and instructed to visit every home all the way around the block until another couple met us from the opposite direction. We took off down the street, diligently ringing doorbells and knocking. We found very few people at home—probably some hid behind closed curtains. We recorded them in our notebook as a Not-At Home (NH), and we'd call on them another day, probably when it rained. We couldn't go door-to-door in the rain, so we'd pull out our NHs and drive all over creation trying to catch up with people. No one was to be left out because our message was life-saving. I firmly believed it then—I wouldn't have wasted my time otherwise, or anyone else's.

Emma skipped along the sidewalks, careful not to step on the cracks. Finally, she stopped to inspect my face. "You're wearing too much blush," she said.

"I am?" How cute, I thought; cute but embarrassing. I figured she should know, since girls Emma's age have pretty good powers of observation, their sense of tactfulness not yet developed to the point where they'd keep it to themselves, or hem-haw around trying to find a more gentle way of saying it.

She reached into her child-sized book-bag and pulled out a tissue. I rubbed the make-up from my cheeks. She watched me, then squinted and cocked her chin. "Much better," she said. She carefully folded the tissue into a square and slipped it into her coat pocket. Even at nine, she was the world's authority on what people should or shouldn't do, which came from those early years of training in the Watchtower Society, training just like mine.

Thankfully, not many had been at home to see me, the funny, red-cheeked, large-bellied clown standing at their door, a Bible in one hand, *Watchtower* and *Awake!* magazines in the other. Thank God Emma was there!

CHAPTER TWENTY-FIVE
MY MATERNITY BLOUSE OF GOOD FORTUNE

I still recall what I was wearing that first day out in service with Emma. The plaid brown and beige maternity top had puffy short sleeves with white lace on the edges, accompanied by a pleated, toast-colored skirt. Unlike maternity clothing of today, back in the 70's you never had a doubt whether a lady was pregnant or just fat. The premise of the maternity top was tent-like to cover up the belly. Today, the sleekness of a maternity dress accentuates the female human body and its ability to procreate as a work of art. I bought the blouse while browsing the maternity section of a K-Mart on Dixie Highway when my period was three days late—I'd wanted to be pregnant for so long. I'd miscarried several months before (two more would follow throughout my childbearing years). I selected my wardrobe with the full assurance I would be with child again, possibly right now if fate had cooperated.

Oh, but my religion taught me not to believe in fate, or even use the word, which, like *destiny*, was a no-no. Fate did not exist, period. Everything was happenstance, coincidence with no meaning. "Time and unforeseen occurrence befall us all." ~ Ecclesiastes 9:11

Now, bear with me here while I digress a moment to visit a very old memory, even before I knew Emma, back when I was a child myself. *Que Sera Sera*, was a popular song sung in the 50's by Doris Day. *Whatever will be, will be, the future's not ours to see, What will be, will be.* My mother warned me there was something fundamentally wrong with those lyrics. She said we did, too, know the future; the Bible told us so. Wasn't that a smidgen contradictory with the time and unforeseen occurrence thing? From then on, I hummed along with the music but I never sang the lyrics. I wondered why it seemed puzzling, but I had already developed the habit of letting the Organization micro-manage my mind. My first red flag had appeared, but, along with many others through the years, I chose to ignore it.

That blouse turned out to be my lucky maternity top. Jehovah's Witness political correctness would dictate it was my *maternity blouse of good fortune*. We didn't believe in luck. No such thing—just good fortune. Semantics were of high priority in the Organization.

Emma and I went out in service together every month. Although too shy to talk to any householders, she was polite, well-mannered and a nice

71

service companion to have, particularly for a nine year old. At the Kingdom Hall, during conversations with other congregation members, I'd turn to see Emma right by my side. She stood next to me as my picture was taken with my decorated cake at the baby shower, insisted on helping me cut the cake and open my presents.

I love it when I associate the *fortunate* blouse with Emma. It hangs in my closet to this day. Occasionally, I caress the fabric, draw it close to my face, attempting to breathe in scents from the past, since *unfortunately* I lost Emma. Her death came five and one-half years after the ugly cantaloupe cyst removal. Three weeks later, I turned my back on The Truth.

CHAPTER TWENTY-SIX
THE FAMILY OF "J"s

Jesse was born in April, and within a couple of months I'd talked Mom into having her mobile home delivered to a lot in Louisville. It didn't take much discussion to get her to move closer to her only grandson. Mom pioneered with the Woodlawn Congregation and found them to be just as welcoming as I had. The following year we were delighted to find ourselves expecting our second son, Jason. If you're following closely you will hear our "J" family—Jim, Joanna, Jesse and Jason. We handled that well until our last son Jordan was born, and I've remained tongue-tied ever since. We didn't plan to do the "J" thing on purpose, but Jim's siblings were named Jack, JoAnn and Jerry, so it may have been subliminal.

Jason was due in 1975, the exact year the Organization strongly suggested the Battle of Armageddon would be fought. According to certain Bible prophesies, interpreted by the men who wrote the *Watchtower* magazine, Armageddon would destroy all wicked and usher in a Paradise Earth. They had discovered data, by reading "between the lines," that we would be in Paradise shortly after 1975. The Biblical proof was all circumstantial, but evidence nonetheless. Every month, we were encouraged to count down another month until we were finally in the new Garden of Eden! With less than a year to go, some congregation members questioned my motives for allowing myself to be happy about expecting a baby during the "time of the end" and I merely explained for a certainty Jehovah could handle those who needed a little extra protection. If their faith had been strong they would've known it themselves. Life goes on.

Preparing for our second child, Jim and I moved from our rented townhouse and bought our first real home. We'd crossed an invisible boundary line again which necessitated changing congregations. I made friends in my new Fairdale Hall, but I didn't see Emma very often for the next three or four years, usually only a couple of times each year at our Circuit Assemblies. I was occupied raising two young sons, and Emma somehow made it through her pre-teen years without me. One important achievement I made during that time was losing my inhibitions and enjoying sex. It was like falling off a mountain and landing safely in Jim's arms. I wished I hadn't wasted ten years before figuring it out.

Four years later, we'd outgrown our starter home. We located a two-story on Second Street in Old Louisville, back in Woodlawn's territory. Built in 1914, the house boasted tall ceilings, original solid walnut doors and woodwork, twelve rooms, three baths, and over 5,000 square feet. As the realtor showed us through, we came to a very large room with windows all across the back in the rear of the second floor. It housed a kitchenette and half-bath and had its own entrance.

I gasped. "Oh, we could turn this into an apartment for Mom."

"I was thinking I'd put a pool table up here," Jim said.

I gave him "the look" and he said, "Just kidding."

We relished the opportunity for home restoration and created a cozy, yet airy apartment for my mother.

My grandma had lived upstairs in our house when I was very little. One day when Mom came home from work, I excitedly ran to her, showing her how Grandma had taught me to tie my shoelaces. Mom cried; *she'd* wanted to teach me herself. Now, I figured since she lived with us, I'd let her teach my sons to tie their shoes to make it up to her. It was really satisfying to me to have her live so close to us, in the same house, and I considered it a blessing that my children would be able to see her every day.

Shortly after we moved in, I knelt beside Jesse for his bedtime prayer. "Mommy," Jesse said. "I want to serve Jehovah because I want to live in Paradise." He must have felt like I did when I was his age. I've quoted him exactly because I wrote it down in my dairy. I hadn't let the fact that I'd lost my earlier diaries stop me from starting current ones. Those new diaries have been a large part of my research for this memoir, in fact, and now that Jesse is an adult, he reads them occasionally.

Jesse always saved part of his weekly allowance. When he was eight, I had a dreadful summer cold, so he dug into his savings and walked with Jason through the neighborhood to a grocery store to buy three long-stemmed red roses. Even though Jason didn't contribute, because he'd spent his allowance the day we gave it to him, Jesse generously claimed the roses were from both of them. The happiness I felt when they presented me with that white flower box lasts to this day. I keep a photo of it on my desk.

With her new apartment in our home, Mom didn't worry with bills, maintenance or anything other than pioneering, which she'd committed to the year after my dad died. I drew even closer to my mother. After Dad's death, I'd come to realize it might be necessary for me to look after her needs as she aged. With her in our home, I easily could take care of anything she required in the future. She stayed at home with both boys while Jim and I went out occasionally. JWs discouraged us from involvement with pop culture, and we rarely attended concerts, but when Harry Chapin came to Louisville in 1979, we took advantage of the built-in babysitter factor. Mom told me not to refer to her as a babysitter because she received pleasure from every moment spent with her grandsons. She took them bowling, hiking in a local park and on half-day train excursions. I hoped to someday be as incredible a grandmother as she was.

At our first meeting back at Woodlawn, Emma ran over to me, squeezed me tight, and whispered *"Welcome home!"* She introduced her boyfriend, Thomas, a quiet young man who couldn't seem to take his eyes off Emma. I didn't blame him—she was a beauty, but she'd changed drastically since I'd last seen her. Approaching fifteen, she wore a heavy dose of eye shadow, profuse mascara, intense red lipstick, and a short skirt and black leather jacket. We sat in the row of seats behind Emma and Thomas. Her hair was styled with the latest fad cut—a shag! Oh, how the *Awake!* magazine had repeatedly warned us against following fads, as it gave us a worldly appearance, and we wouldn't want anyone to think we were part of this world now would we? Even though we lived in the world didn't mean we should copy or enjoy it, and if we did, well . . . it shouldn't be obvious.

The youthful lovebirds cuddled and whispered throughout the entire meeting, paying no attention to the scriptural admonition offered from the platform. It was rather distracting and I was somewhat gloomy, thinking Emma had become so *worldly* without my motherly guidance. I recalled the day she'd told me I had too much blush on.

She must have sensed my thoughts—turned and smiled at me with those haunting green eyes of hers—and I smiled back. I never uttered one word of criticism; by this time I had lived long enough to grasp the futility of criticizing others. I imagined Lydia was having fits with her, though, and her father, too, being an elder and all—how embarrassing for him. I figured the elders were probably all over him for not keeping his teenage daughter in check.

Now, as I reminisce, I smile. Emma was merely expressing herself as a human being in spite of all obstacles. She used the methods most teenagers do to find their own identity: make-up, hairstyle and accessories—tame compared to worldly girls—no tattoos or piercings for Emma! And now I have to laugh, because I thought I would *never* have such problems with my own kids. I smugly knew I was a much better parent than anyone else. You see, I was still somewhat of a know-it-all. I should have seen the signs, and I would have . . . if I'd been paying more attention.

What signs? One evening, Jesse and Jason, by then six and eight, had been invited to come up on stage during a Thursday night Service Meeting with all the other kids in the congregation. Elder Christophe was going to show parents how to encourage their offspring to serve God full-time after they grew up, (in case Armageddon hadn't shown up by then, since it was already six years late) to inculcate that desire in them while they were very young. The children were not informed about the questions they would be asked.

Elder Christophe asked Jesse what he wanted to be when he grew up, and then stuck a microphone in his face. "A cowboy," Jesse said without hesitation.

The audience chuckled. Jason was asked the question. "I'm gonna be an Indian," he stated with surety.

The entire thing could have been scripted it was so funny and spontaneous! The audience howled. I wanted to sink down into my chair and disappear. Obviously our parenting methods weren't working and now the entire congregation would be aware of it.

Elder Christophe inquired the same from his daughter, and wouldn't you know she wanted to be a pioneer. Wasn't that peachy? I'm sure *she* had no coaching from her parents at home before the meeting. "So, brothers and sisters, here on our left is the "J" family, to show us the wrong way, and on our right is *my* family showing you the acceptable way to raise your children."

Elder Christophe didn't say that—he didn't have to.

Well.

I am far removed from the Organization now, so I have no idea, nor do I give a rip, but in all probability Elder Christophe's daughter did turn out to be Little Miss Perfect Witness.

Jesse and Jason never developed the desire to pioneer, but they showed respect to those who did. They are, in fact, playful cowboys and Indians, and at other times guitarists, heavy metal rockers, skaters, carpenters, drinkers, and most important of all now: adult college students and sober fathers—out in the world, despite all the fruitless times I spent knocking my head against a brick wall teaching them what I believed to be the best, the *only* way to everlasting life through Jehovah's Christian Organization.

CHAPTER TWENTY-SEVEN
LET'S DECORATE!

The congregation had grown and the little Woodlawn Kingdom Hall and its postage stamp-sized parking lot were too small. One family donated a sizeable piece of land adjacent to their home a few miles away; ground-breaking and construction took off. I had a flair for color and décor, so the elders added me to the Decorating Committee. It was my job to survey paint and wallpaper stores and to provide samples for the elders' final decision. I asked Emma and Lydia to accompany me and was pleased to discover the three of us had a similar sense of style. We walked into Sherwin Williams with a pair of scissors and a small scrapbook. When we found a potential color, we taped the color chip to one page and on the opposite page wallpaper samples with the prices per roll written to one side. There were several rooms to decorate: men's and women's restroom, mother's room, conference room, the main hall and the stage, and everything had to coordinate.

"The elders want a traditional look," I said.

Emma's expression showed her distaste. "*They* would!"

"It *is* a place of worship, you know," Lydia said.

"Yeah, right," Emma giggle-snorted, which led me to do the same.

Lydia sighed and shook her head as if to say, "Where did I go wrong?"

We selected a pale blue and ivory theme and the elders approved. Emma and I shopped for light fixtures and conventional-style chairs for the raised, front platform. We fell in love with two chairs that were too expensive for the congregation's budget, so I talked Jim into buying them. Everything had to be perfectly matched to make Emma and me happy. The chairs were to be used when sisters gave their Ministry School talks and for other demonstrations during the Service Meetings. We chose silk flower arrangements for the stage and once the Hall was built, we measured walls, ordered wallpaper and spent several days hanging the stuff. We had each papered our own places so many times, we were professional hangers by most standards. Emma couldn't live for more than one year at a time without changing her bedroom décor! Once the last strip of paper was hung, she'd browse decorating magazines for the next look she wanted. She was peculiar that way, one of the many things I loved about her.

After we completed our decorating job, we went in field service

77

together every week. Lydia, Emma, my mother and I would spend a morning knocking on doors, then we'd hit a Mexican restaurant for lunch and later drag Emma along as we shopped for antiques, but she preferred the clothing bargains at the Fashion Shop. She'd outgrown her need to wear a black leather jacket to the Kingdom Hall. She'd helped decorate it and wanted an appropriate appearance for herself.

The elders chose floor coverings and upholstery fabric for the donated theater chairs they'd retrieved from an old movie palace in town. We had gone to lunch and returned to the Hall to see if the carpet installation was finished.

"What on earth?" Emma nearly screamed.

"What's wrong?"

"Would you look at this?" She dug from her purse the carpet swatch we'd been carrying around with us for weeks and threw it to the floor. It landed upside down. I bent over and turned it right side up. I saw in an instant what had upset her. The carpet they'd sent from Dalton, Georgia did not match the sample, thus it did not *exactly* coordinate with any of the paper we'd so carefully hung. "Surely they will do something about this, don't you think?" Emma said. I laughed under my breath and said, "What do *you* think?"

Finally everything was complete, and we held a Dedication Program for our brand new Woodlawn Kingdom Hall. Everyone, including Emma and I, had gone door-to-door inviting the neighbors to come and see what we were all about. The hall was packed with people from all over. We were two of the first to arrive, and we paid close attention to everyone mingling and admiring the beautiful interior.

"No one seems to notice the carpet fiasco," I whispered.

Emma smirked in reply, "Most of the congregation members definitely lack our style of discerning taste."

My mother donated her Hammond organ and she played as the congregation sang along. She would be invited to play for several weddings, Emma's brother, Bryan's, being one of them.

Soon, another wedding was held, but my mom couldn't play the organ for it. She was to be the bride!

CHAPTER TWENTY-EIGHT
A HAND-PICKED STEP-FATHER

Jim's Aunt Martha passed away suddenly in the spring of 1979, leaving his Uncle Enos alone and depressed. Enos and Martha had been Witnesses since early adulthood, and they had followed the Organization's request in the 1940's to put off having children until the earth was transformed into a paradise. Oops—Enos had no children to comfort him—only nieces and nephews, Jim being one of several.

I asked my three sisters-in-law what they thought about getting my mom and Enos together.

"Do you realize how stubborn he is?" JoAnn said.

"I think it's a brilliant idea." Barbara, Jerry's wife said.

Lois, Jackie's wife, agreed. Mom had been widowed for eleven years by then, and she and Enos had much in common, especially religion. I figured Mom could hold her own as far as stubbornness was concerned. The only problem was Mom. She insisted she was not interested in meeting him except for friendship. *Hmmm. We'll see about that*, I thought.

While still in Indianapolis, she'd previously turned down two potential suitors because, even though she tried, she couldn't find an attraction to either one. A third one surfaced shortly after she'd moved to Louisville. Same result—no appeal. Those experiences led her to realize how much she valued living alone. She'd been married to my dad for twenty-seven years, and I'd often wondered how she managed to keep a smile on her face on the days when his alcohol addiction was in full force. Single life was good for her now: no one to worry about, pick up after, or cook for; less laundry and no distractions other than those two cute grandsons living one floor below. She enjoyed entertaining and attending social functions with her friends. She was often invited to accompany JW families on vacations and she cherished her wonderful, single life.

However, I'd known Enos Kimball fourteen years. He was different from the rest and would make her life even more wonderful! He was an elder in the Anderson, Indiana congregation, and they were both sixty-five. At that age, how much time should one waste? They didn't wait long—Enos and Mom married on June 8, 1980.

The "cupid" process took less than six months. I'd asked my sisters-in-law to help me coax Enos down to Louisville for an anniversary get-together for Jim's parents in December. He rode with Jackie and Lois and was unaware they would be spending the night. We trapped the poor man because we were afraid he'd refuse to come if he found out it was for the entire weekend. I introduced him to my mother, and it wasn't long before they were engrossed in conversation, oblivious to everyone else in the house. We all smiled at one another because we knew what we were up to, even though Mom and Enos didn't have a clue. But they followed the theme of the plot just as though they knew it was their destiny.

Two months later, I asked Enos to come back to our home with the plea that JoAnn's car was unreliable and she needed a ride so we could go see Mikhail Baryshnikov dance with the Louisville Ballet. Enos obliged as he loved JoAnn dearly and wanted to be helpful. They stayed for three days, during which time JoAnn and I busied ourselves with shopping excursions and other excuses to leave him with my mother. They went in the ministry together, and he insisted on going to her old mobile home. She'd mentioned it had a loose door knob and he was eager to fix it.

Before he left for home that week, my mother breathlessly confided in me that she was terribly smitten with him, but she didn't think he looked at her that way. "What should I do?" she said.

It was time for an intervention.

On the Wednesday morning Enos was to take JoAnn home, I asked him to sit down with me in the dining room with some coffee. "I want to talk to you about something important," I said, "but I'm afraid you'll be upset with me."

"There's nothing you could say that would upset me. What is it?"

I took a breath and thought, *here goes!* "Well . . . it's probably much too soon after Martha's death last year, but I am hoping that maybe someday you and my mother will get together." *There, I've gone and done it!*

"I see," Enos said with an expressionless face. "I don't think your mother has any intention of remarriage. She seems content to me."

Oh great. I had no choice but to spill the beans. "Yes, she *was* content until she met you, and she will totally kill me if she finds out I've told you this, but, well, she claims she can't get you off her mind!"

Enos' face remained unreadable and I held my breath.

Finally I said, "It's probably too soon for you to even consider it. Just think about it, if you will."

He said he would.

Three days later, he called for two things. One was to thank me for my hospitality, and the other was to ask for my mother's telephone number. "Oh boy!" I said. "You've thought about what I told you, haven't you?"

Enos chuckled. "I've thought of nothing *but* that!"

I wasted no time running upstairs to Mom's apartment to fill her in on the latest. She was beyond thrilled, and within a few minutes her telephone rang. I wiggled my eyebrows and left her apartment; I'd hear the scoop soon enough.

For the next few weeks they spent countless, expensive long-distance hours on the telephone. The next time Enos drove down to Louisville was for the express purpose of visiting my mother without anyone making up an excuse. As soon as she opened the door, he pulled her into his arms, kissed her right on the lips and said, "Will you be my wife?"

I threw a party—a wedding shower, and Emma helped me with the refreshments and typical, yet mandatory, *goofball games,* according to Emma. Lydia made silk flower arrangements for their wedding. I was her matron of honor; Jim walked her down the aisle; Jesse and Jason were the ring bearers. Enos moved from Anderson to live with his new wife in her apartment on the second floor of our home, and shortly thereafter he signed up to pioneer with her.

Jim refused rent from Mom and Enos out of respect for their pioneer service, even though both had an adequate Social Security income. Encouraged by the addition of his pioneering Uncle Enos to the household, Jim increased his meeting attendance and even went in the ministry work on occasion.

College attendance is practically forbidden among Witnesses, but Jim made a good living for his family. Five years previously, he had started Kellems and Coe Tool Corporation and had achieved considerable financial success. At Jim's request, I learned the skill of bookkeeping and worked part-time for him. Jim was a large contributor at the Woodlawn congregation, the "go-to" guy when any purchase above the ordinary was considered, and whenever he showed up at a meeting, the elders wasted no time in welcoming him. While the Organization viewed as suspicious anyone who would seek a college career, they seemed to have no qualms about accepting donations from someone who'd made a success by on-the-job full-time experience, which took much longer than college would have.

CHAPTER TWENTY-NINE
WELCOME TO NEW YORK

In early August, 1982, Jim and I took our two sons to visit Bethel, the Watchtower headquarters in Brooklyn, New York. Not only was the Organization housed there, but thousands of brothers and sisters lived and worked at Bethel, voluntarily performing all sorts of tasks, mostly publishing the Society's literature. Some served as bookbinders, copy editors, cooks, waiters, maintenance workers and so on. They received a small monthly stipend for essentials and were given free room and board, including medical and dental treatment. A couple we'd known since our teens, Joe and Sandy, had been members of the Bethel family for many years. They invited us to stay in the Standish Arms, a hotel owned by the Society, free to selected guests of the Bethel family. Armageddon was now seven years late, but at least it gave us a chance to tour the facilities before the world came to an end. Sandy and Joe said most folks housed there thought it would be the safest place when Armageddon hit. We felt a little more comfortable being so close to the *safe house* during our vacation.

Sandy took a day off and accompanied Jim and I as we showed our sons much of Manhattan via sidewalks and subways. Jesse pointed to an ad on the train for the insecticide, Roach Motel, and said, "Look! That's where we're staying." The night before, we'd returned to our room and turned on the lights. Welcome to New York.

We took in the main tourist attractions: Fifth Avenue, Rockefeller Center, Harlem, Central Park, Macy's, The Empire State Building and the Staten Island Ferry. We ended our day with Sandy at Mr. Souvlacki's, a vintage Greek diner. Later, Joe took us on a midnight tour. At the World Trade Center, Joe slipped his car into a spot marked "No Parking" and we zipped up the elevator to the top lookout for an extraordinary view. We were uneasy when we felt the building sway, but Joe said the towers were designed to be flexible due to their excessive height. The Big Apple glittered with pride after dark.

The remainder of our eight-day vacation consisted of an upstate New York winery tour and Niagara Falls. Traveling through Pennsylvania on our way home, we enjoyed Hershey Park where Jason tasted his first "big-person's" rollercoaster ride. The aroma of chocolate wafted over the town of

Hershey where the street lights were shaped like Kisses.

The first day at home, I went through our stack of mail, came across a Cruise Travel magazine, and started planning our next vacation. However, it would have to wait, because a few days later I realized I was pregnant. When I wasn't experiencing morning sickness, I was too sleepy to accomplish anything productive. I had previously signed up to auxiliary pioneer in September (60 hours per month, one month at a time), but my altered condition prevented me from going in the ministry work day after day. I asked the elders to withdraw my application, but they claimed it couldn't be done. One elder instructed me to spend my time writing letters at home—to people in the phone book! I silently labeled him as a moron who obviously had no firsthand knowledge of pregnancy or hormonal women.

At seven weeks I miscarried. Jim and I spent most of that day in the Out-Patient Department of Norton Hospital, only a few blocks from Jesse and Jason's school. Jim had the sad task of meeting them after school and explaining the situation. He walked with them to the hospital, and Jason ran to my bedside, crying. He was the most disappointed of all four of us—he'd wanted a baby brother or sister so much; he hugged me over and over. They presented me with a gold-foil box of Godiva chocolates and we each sampled the delicacies, but really nothing would soothe the grief of our loss except time. But how much time did I have?

Twelve days later on October 5, I turned thirty-five, officially at a turning point, I thought. I was compelled—nearly obsessed—to figure out what to do next with my life. My sons spent their days in elementary school, so would I be expected to pioneer full-time? Mom and Enos suggested I give it a try, but what I'd always wanted was a daughter and my "mommy hormones" were talking to me.

During the weeks between our New York trip, and then my miscarriage and feeble attempts to spend sixty hours of service time in September, Emma and Thomas were married. I have no recollection of a wedding, so I can only assume they went to the court house and made it official. It all happened very fast, like before I knew it, zip, she changed her last name. I assumed the early marriage was because they wanted to have sex, like the rest of us. I don't know if that's why they married while she was still underage, but it was a big influence on why Jim and I rushed into it at eighteen.

If a Jehovah's Witness has sex with someone they're not married to, it's an automatic disfellowshipping offense. While it's tempting to sneak around, why risk losing your friends and family when all you have to do is simply make it legal? Many couples arbitrarily marry young in the

Organization, only to find they've made a commitment to someone not suited to them in any way. The only thing they had in common was their religion and urgent libido. If one of them opts out of the religion, as is often the case, they either remain unhappily married, or divorce and both leave The Truth, heading into the world for a better life. As it turned out, Emma and Thomas had a long and happy time together and I greatly admired their relationship. She loved him dearly and was faithful and true all the way to the end.

The day before Thanksgiving, I discovered I'd been successful in my attempt to become pregnant again, but I didn't broadcast it because of the miscarriage two months earlier. By late December, I was ready to announce it to the world. After a meeting at the Kingdom Hall, Emma came up to me and tearfully asked for a hug.

"What's wrong, honey?" I said.

"I'm pregnant." Emma said, "I just found out, and I didn't want to have a baby this soon. I'm only seventeen and I haven't a clue how to do this."

I held her close, and whispered in her ear, "Guess what? I'm pregnant too!"

Emma blinked and the tears rolled down her cheeks. "Can we do this together?" she asked.

"Why not? I think we definitely should!"

My baby was due in late July and Emma's in August. We shopped for maternity clothes, baby clothes, fabric and wallpaper for our nurseries. We decided to decorate them somewhat alike. We lunched at our favorite Mexican restaurant and talked about nursing bras and homemade baby food. We both fell in love with a baby stroller at Toys"R"Us. They had only two left, so we put them in layaway. She asked what she could do to avoid stretch marks and I laughed. My first two babies were over nine pounds each, and stretch marks were the least of my worries by then. Having my third child at thirty-five was more physically challenging than the first two in my twenties. My feet were swollen and it was hard to keep up with Emma at the mall!

Emma gave me a baby shower and I threw one for her. All the same people attended, but we didn't have a double shower because we each wanted to be the center of attention at our own! When Jordan was born four weeks late, Emma whined on the telephone—it was so unfair that I would finally have my baby while hers was late getting here too! Ten days later, Anthony was born—Emma and Thomas were thrilled with their son; I wasn't the least bit disappointed to have another boy, because I had a daughter in Emma, after all.

CHAPTER THIRTY

I REALLY MISSED THE EASTER BUNNY

There is not one single, worldly holiday Jehovah's Witnesses are allowed to celebrate. They all have "pagan origins," a supposed fact the Organization apparently researched in depth. I learned this while my mother was studying the Bible with Bill and Jeanette Hastings. I asked one of my infamous, life-altering questions: "How can we know for sure Jesus was born on December twenty-fifth?"

Oops, turns out he wasn't. "Everyone knows that," Brother Hastings said. "Check out a Catholic encyclopedia. It will have an accurate and thorough history of the holiday and its origin."

My mother investigated right away. She said since it wasn't really the day of Christ's birth we would stop celebrating Christmas immediately. What a bummer! I loved the scent of a fresh evergreen tree in the living room, aglow with bubble lights, strings of popcorn and tinsel, the train running around in a circle underneath surrounded by presents! And get this: December twenty-fifth was my dad's birthday, but he simply lit a Camel, popped the top off another Schlitz, and said, *"Christ-My-Ass,* it's all about commercialism anyway." He'd said this about Christmas for years, so his indifference to Mom's refusal to celebrate came as no surprise. His parents, brother and sisters took it in stride, shaking their heads while murmuring polite, whispered questions I overheard: *What has she gotten herself into? Do you think maybe it's a phase she's going through?*

Then, all of a sudden, we didn't celebrate birthdays at all, not even *mine!* Something about John the Baptist's head being chopped off at a pagan birthday party, and, at a prostitute's request, served on a silver platter. Well, *I* still felt special on my birthday, but I was no longer allowed to have my neighborhood friends in for a party. No cake, no presents. I wrote *Happy Birthday, Joanna* in my diary each year on the fifth day of October. (I wonder if a Hoosier farmer ever read it.)

No candy hearts on Valentine's Day, no fireworks on the Fourth of July, no ghost costumes on Halloween, no turkey on Thanksgiving Day, and no more banging pots and pans together on our front porch at midnight to welcome in the New Year. If you're counting, there were five "no's" in the previous sentence alone, and it didn't even include Christmas or Easter!

~*~

It pained me to lose the Easter Bunny. I had a special place in my heart for her, and not because of the lovely pastel colors of the spring holiday or the milk chocolate. It had more to do with rabbit ears.

We were three and four months pregnant the day I introduced Emma to a Palmer's solid chocolate Easter bunny. It was the day after Valentine's Day, and I knew from experience that Consolidated, a discount store before the Target or Wal-Mart era, would scoot the Valentine stuff onto clearance tables and set up their Easter candy display.

Emma and I and my boys pulled into the parking lot when the store opened at exactly ten o'clock, and while the other customers rushed for the clearance table, we went straight for the Easter aisle. My fingers quickly glided by the yellow chicks and the colorful jelly beans. I grabbed a twelve-inch Palmer solid chocolate bunny and handed it to Emma.

"You'll find Paradise when you bite the ears off this sucker, honey," I said.

She giggled and her green eyes glistened. "This reminds me of Adam and Eve." She turned it over to check the label. The Society had informed us that Lecithin, a blood derivative, was an ingredient of finer chocolates, and if we knowingly ate it, *that* would keep us out of Paradise. Our religion did not permit us to ingest blood in any way. Thus, reading candy labels was a requirement. If we unknowingly ate a blood derivative, would we make it into Paradise by default? Or, was ignorance no excuse?

I handed a bunny to Jesse and Jason and selected one for myself. We rushed to the cashier, hoping we wouldn't run into anyone who knew us, then hurried to the car and ripped open our prizes, counted to three and we bit our bunny's ears in unison.

"This has *gotta* be sinful!" Emma said with her mouth full.

"Yeah!" Jason said from the backseat.

"What's sinful about it?" Jesse asked.

"Easter is a Pagan holiday, child," Emma said.

"Sure," Jesse said, "but look—we're not eating Easter candy." He held his chocolate up for all to see. Sure enough, without ears or a head, it was merely a solid chocolate chunk. Oh, the curious mind of a nine-year-old boy.

"Hmmm." Emma bit the tail. "There . . . just plain chocolate now. Mighty good chocolate, too. Not that artificially flavored, waxy stuff."

There was nothing like it, and my grown sons still talk about how we looked forward to the day after Valentine's Day. Consolidated is no longer in business and Palmer seems to have discontinued their large, solid chocolate bunnies. Sure, there's always an overabundance of hollow ones, but, let's face it: there is no valid, worthwhile substitute for a large, solid chocolate rabbit with big ears.

"Did you ever celebrate Easter?" Emma asked.

"For the first eight years of my life we did," I said.

"I don't remember ever having it," Emma said.

"My basket was woven with yellow, pink and pale green wicker; wide, blue satin ribbons were tied into bows at the handle."

"Ah . . . Easter colors for sure," Emma said.

"Of course, what was inside the basket was what really mattered. My mother layered the bottom with shredded pink crepe paper, then scattered jelly beans all around. It was like an outdoor egg hunt, digging my little fingers into the Easter grass to find them. The yellow sugar-coated marshmallow chicks in cellophane wrappings were next, then an assortment of hollow eggs wrapped in colorful foil. Around the edges, she'd carefully placed the hard-boiled eggs we'd dyed and decorated the day before, but I wasn't interested in eating those. They were there for the artisan effect—the tradition. The main centerpiece, as you might guess, was a huge, solid milk chocolate rabbit. I think Mom spent a fortune on those baskets."

"Well . . . you were an only child, you lucky dog . . . I mean you fortunate dog!"

Jesse said, "I wish I was an only child."

Through my rearview mirror I saw Jason punch Jesse on the arm and Jesse, of course, pretended to be severely injured.

I turned to the backseat and said, "Calm down! Eat your chocolate and be quiet." Quite the oxymoron, I realized after I'd given the order. The candy's sugar content would undoubtedly prevent the effect for which I'd asked.

"Anyway," I continued, "Mom had the habit of hiding my basket on the floor, behind the drapes at our living room window. I always spied the obvious bulge on my way into the kitchen for breakfast."

"So you knew right where to look. That's not much fun," Emma said.

"I *made* it fun, though," I said.

"How?" Jason asked.

"After breakfast, when the last dish had been rinsed and placed into the drainer to dry, Mom pretended to see something outside the kitchen window, and she'd say, 'Oh! Did you see that?'

"Dad said he thought maybe he did see something. He even claimed to hear a noise coming from the living room, but he guessed it was Nopi."

"Nopi was your dog, right?" Emma asked.

87

"Yes, and that was my cue. I'd tell them Nopi was down the basement, unless they'd let her out already. Then, one or the other of them would suddenly remember, yes, they let Nopi out earlier, so, no, the noise couldn't have come from her."

I bit the top half of my bunny's head and let it dissolve in my mouth before I continued my story. "I watched them going back and forth with their drama and I sighed. I knew if I were patient, eventually they'd get around to telling me they thought perhaps, just perhaps, the Easter Bunny had visited and maybe we should look around to see if she'd left anything behind. Oh, do you think so?"

Emma laughed and nibbled on the dwindling torso.

"Well, I couldn't ruin their fun and go straight for the living room drapes. I'd open every kitchen cabinet, linen closet, and all the bedroom drawers. I'd look underneath the beds, and they'd follow me the entire time, everywhere I went. I timed it well and finally I'd go for the living room drapes.

"I'd shout, 'Look at this!' I pulled the basket up into my arms and went straight for the chocolate ears. Halfway through the delicacy, I remembered to offer my parents a bite, and out of courtesy they'd take a nibble and advise me not to eat too much all at once."

"Savor it," Mom always said. "Save some for later. Make it last."

"Gretchen is smart," Emma said.

"Yes, and such wise advice it was, because the Easter Bunny decided to skip my house when I was eight years old. She visited all the other kids, but not me. Not anymore."

"That's when Grandma was baptized?" Jesse asked.

"Right around there, yes. And because we had been enlightened about Jesus and how he'd ordered his followers during the last supper to celebrate his death, not his resurrection. So Easter was officially out!"

"That's weird—celebrating death," Jesse said. "How do we do that?"

"At the Memorial," Emma said, "You know . . . where the brothers pass around the unleavened bread and the wine, but only those who believe they're going to heaven when they die partake. Usually nobody." Emma giggled.

Jason said, "I remember. I always like to sniff that wine when it passes by me."

"I do that, too!" Jesse said.

"You're direct descendents of your grandfather," I said with a chuckle. "I mean, I always thought of my dad at the Memorial when I was little. If he'd gone along with us, he would have said, 'What a waste of good booze.'

"Anyway, my neighborhood girlfriends sympathized and offered to share their candy, but I'd say *no thank you*, because I wouldn't dare partake in the spoils of a pagan holiday. It was possible I might not make it to Paradise if I ate chocolate in the shape of an Easter rabbit."

Emma observed what was left of the soft brown torso in her hand. "It's a good thing this is just plain chocolate, then, right?"

By then, I had lost my magical, mystical childhood fears and had decided not to pass them on to my sons. For the most part, I'd developed some common sense. Although, looking back, I can see I could've used a lot more of it.

On the way home, Emma suggested since I liked the Easter Bunny so much, I should use Peter Rabbit as my nursery theme. I thought it was an excellent idea so I went overboard with Beatrix Potter. I found a musical mobile for the baby's crib with several of the author's animal characters attached. Imagine my delight to discover a chic toy store which offered stuffed animals such as Peter Rabbit, Benjamin Bunny and Jeremy Fischer.

When my mother heard of our escapades to Consolidated, she asked me why we had to have a chocolate bunny. "I mean, why an *Easter* bunny? There are plenty of other good, solid chocolates out there."

"Mom," I said, "you don't understand the whole complexity of the situation. It's not necessarily the chocolate, or the bunny, it's the combination of having the ears right up there in front of you, waiting to be attacked. That kind of chocolate tastes better."

"You're right," she said. "I don't get it."

"Well, you don't have to get it. I didn't buy you one, anyway. I knew you wouldn't partake. But, trust me when I say there is nothing wrong with it."

She sighed. "Okay." She made an attempt to change the subject, but when she paused and looked off into the distance, I knew what she was thinking about—her little girl's precious Easter basket from years past.

~*~

There must have been so much chocolate in our blood it seeped into our genes, because my grandson Jackson, Jesse's son, has one requirement while on vacation in St. Augustine: a solid chocolate alligator from Kilwin's Candy Shop. He eats the tail first and must be strongly encouraged before he shares with the rest of us. There is something to be said about the pleasure of biting body parts off of solid chocolate animals. Even my vegetarian granddaughter Greta, Jason's daughter, doesn't have a problem with it. And we never check labels on our chocolate to see if the candy contains Lecithin.

Who cares?

My house sits in the middle of two acres, half of which is woods. We cleared a winding pathway where we hide goodie-filled plastic eggs on either side. Greta and Jackson saunter along the path, collecting eggs and dropping them into little bags we decorated earlier with crayons and stickers. Where the path ends at our Secret Garden, they find their Easter baskets filled with even more candy. Jesse and Jason follow and laugh, joining their children in the reverie, and I take videos and pictures and wish my sons could've had this adventure as children. I'd raised them in The Truth, but fortunately for all of us, it didn't take! They're free to worship as they chose, or not.

It's true, it *is* better to give than receive, and when I watch their escapades my happiness is immeasurable. I'm sure I feel like my parents did when they tagged along while I searched for my basket.

I missed the Easter Bunny the most when I was a kid, even more than Santa Claus, but now I miss Emma more than anything.

CHAPTER THIRTY-ONE
MOTHER'S DAY

When I awakened on Mother's Day, muted sounds of Mom and Enos, getting ready for the meeting, filtered through the ceiling above my bed. I hopped up and fixed breakfast for my family. Emma and I were six and seven months along by then. After the meeting, I found my way across the Kingdom Hall and whispered in her ear, "Do you feel somehow . . . special today?"

"No. Why? Should I?"

"It's Mother's Day," I said matter-of-factly.

"Oh . . . yeah, but we don't celebrate it."

"So it means nothing to you?"

"Not really," she said with indifference.

"I'll bet next year you'll feel differently . . . when you're a mother yourself."

"No I won't, you goofball!"

~*~

It is Mother's Day as I write this. I awakened to a room filled with sunshine and I stretched, happy to be a mother, thought of each of my three sons and how I've enjoyed motherhood so much. Then, I thought of my own mother. I went to the computer and wrote a tribute to her on Facebook.

> "For Gretchen: I miss you so much today. I relish the memory of that scrumptious hug you brought to me in a dream last month. I even wrote a story about it. Thank you for encouraging me to become a writer. You have influenced my life in so many ways, just as you said I've done for you. We were quite a team. I think we still are, even though you don't live right next door anymore. Your only daughter, Joanna"

I think today of the entire time I had my mother by my side, over forty-eight years, and I never once acknowledged her on Mother's Day. Why didn't I? As I recall, the Organization proclaimed that Mother's Day, like any other fun holiday, had pagan origins—something about worship of the mother—whatever. At Exodus 20:12 the bible says, "Honor your father and your mother in order that your days may prove long upon the ground that Jehovah your God is giving you." So, why not honor her on Mother's Day? Why on one certain day each year could we not?

It was the same on Thanksgiving Day—the Organization said we should be thankful every day, so not to pick one special day to celebrate. No Thanksgiving dinner for us, unless, of course, we had turkey, dressing, yams, pumpkin pie and hot, buttered yeast rolls every other day of the year, as well.

Only God should be worshiped, all others could be honored. Evidently, if we acknowledged Mother's day we weren't honoring our mother, we were actually worshipping her.

I know—it makes no sense to me either.

CHAPTER THIRTY-TWO
FATHER'S DAY

Since Emma hadn't felt special on Mother's Day, I knew she would breeze right past Father's Day without a thought, so I didn't bring it up. My father had been gone fourteen years by then.

~*~

More than forty-three years have passed now, as I write this. On Father's Day I posted this tribute to my dad on Facebook:

"Father's Day: My dad, Charles, died in 1969 at the age of 51 of a myocardial infarction. I was twenty-one at the time. Although he struggled with alcoholism all of his life, he never failed to show his love for me. He called me a Princess, so naturally I always knew I was one. That's where my attitude comes from in case any of you wondered. Yep, it's from my daddy."

~*~

I had a dream about my dad recently. When I awakened, I cried—I'd taken his military service for granted, more worried about what people would think of the flag and the Navy's presence at the cemetery.

Uncle Howard died a few years ago and his three daughters held a celebration party for him. They asked me if I'd like to speak, along with several others, and I was happy to do so. After the service, Naval officers in full dress stood at attention, rifles at an angle. The twenty-one gun salute. Tears flowed from the memories of my father and for the love of Uncle Howard.

I watched my cousins—Tracey, Tina and Toby—after they'd received the triangular-shaped flag. They formed an intimate circle, laughing and crying, caressing the cloth with the same fondness as when they'd touched their father's weary face, moments before he passed away.

A wave of shame washed through me. We'd discarded Dad's flag without a second thought, having been programmed to remain neutral, to feel nothing other than disdain for anything that was a part of the world.

I wish I had the flag, and Dad's blue navy uniform, too. I remember wearing it for Halloween as a child, before we stopped celebrating that horribly pagan, Satanic ritual called trick-or-treating. My three sons would be happy to have the flag and uniform in our memory box. They were born after Dad's death, so they never had the opportunity to know him.

A black and white photograph of him standing at attention in his uniform, rifle at his side, hangs on a wall in my home office.

CHAPTER THIRTY-THREE
THEY SAID IT WAS A MIRACLE

"Doubt may be the most civilizing force we have available to us, for it is doubt that protects us from the arrogance of utter rightness, from the barbarism of blind loyalties, all of which threaten the human possibility." ~ Rabbi Leonard Beerman

"There lives more faith in honest doubt, believe me, than in half the creeds." ~ Alfred Lord Tennyson

Jordan Tyler Coe was born on August 21, 1983, mid-afternoon, after twelve hours of labor. His father and brothers, wearing scrubs and masks, were invited to follow me into the delivery room. The all-in-one "birthing room" had not yet become popular. All was going according to plan until the last few minutes.

Mom, in the waiting room down the hall, became alarmed when she heard an announcement over the surgery department PA system for all emergency personnel to report to delivery room #2 STAT.

They'd given me an epidural too soon, even though fully aware the baby was exceptionally large. I was told to push, but I didn't have adequate control of my abdominal muscles. Two nurses climbed up on my bed, one on either side, and literally pushed on my uterus, putting the infant under distress. In the birth canal, he took a breath through his nostrils, drawing liquid into his lungs. His head delivered, but his body wouldn't budge because his shoulders were as large as a fully-suited football player.

A fetal monitor alerted the medical team that the baby's heart rate dropped to the danger level. My Obstetrician's name was Lyman G. Armstrong, M. D., a short, stout fellow with stubby fingers which simply wouldn't accommodate a manipulation of the infant's shoulders out of the birth canal. He was about to break the baby's clavicle to fold his shoulders into a deliverable size, when a *very* tall doctor ran into the room, and with the use of his long, slender fingers, easily managed to complete the baby's delivery. Jordan was not breathing and was immediately wrapped up like a mummy in gauze and whisked away into a neo-natal procedure room where his lungs were intubated and drained. None of us in the family saw his face or held him. What a relief it was when we heard the news that the eleven pound, eight ounce baby boy was breathing on his own.

During the last half of my pregnancy, I'd held a Norman Rockwell type of image in my mind. My husband and sons would be there by my side while the baby was effortlessly delivered. The boys would experience the beauty of childbirth and hold their newborn sibling if they wanted to. Jim would catch it all on film. So much for my dream. Jim ushered Jesse and Jason out of the delivery room, and I was numb, wishing they hadn't been there to see that last-minute fiasco.

Jordan spent the next five days in the neo-natal nursery. He looked like a giant compared to the miniature premature infants in their incubators alongside him. Dr. Armstrong confided they should've done a Caesarean Section since they realized he was so large and one month overdue. Hindsight. One would think a medical doctor would have the intelligence to use foresight; however it was the custom to see Dr. Armstrong on one pre-delivery visit, and Dr. Hyman on the next. Dr. Hyman had seen me last, and his response to my question, "How is this huge baby going to get out of me?" was this: "Your pelvis is made for large babies. Don't worry about a thing. He won't weigh over ten pounds at the most."

"*She* won't?" I corrected him. I was going to have a girl, and that was that. He reminded me of the imbecile I'd seen after three months of marriage who told me to relax and not worry about climaxing during sex.

But that wasn't the end of it. My uterus, six weeks short of its thirty-sixth birthday, decided to rebel, and really can you blame the old gal? It was stretched beyond capacity to retract; non-stop bleeding was evident within the hour after they wheeled me to recovery. I dozed, awakening when I was given the news that baby Jordan had sufficiently recovered, was breathing normally, and didn't seem to have suffered any permanent damage. I fell asleep again, a happy new mother. I awakened only slightly when nurses massaged my abdominal muscles, encouraging the uterus to retract.

Medical personnel filled the room. Jim stood in the rear corner. He appeared to be crying. Where were my sons and my mother? In the waiting room down the hall, someone informed me.

"Your vital signs have taken a nose dive and you've gone into congestive heart failure," my nurse said. "Will you accept a blood transfusion?"

The word "no" slipped out of my mouth without a second thought. What to do in case of an emergency was ingrained in me—just say no.

A final appeal from my nurse: "Do you realize your life is in danger?"

I replied with a yes to that one, but the pain meds running through my IV made it all seem like a Disney movie destined for a happy ending. My bed-on-wheels sped out of the recovery room as I watched ceiling tiles and fluorescent lights whiz by on the way to surgery. I summoned enough presence of mind to pray to Jehovah, "Please let me live. I have three sons to raise."

Doctor Armstrong packed the uterus with absorbent fabric. My vital signs stabilized and I returned to the recovery area. When I awakened, my nurse was by my side. I asked, "Did I die?" She laughed and said, "If you did, this would surely be heaven, and I pray to God heaven is *not* like this place!"

Soon, my mother and sons entered, along with Jim, having survived the fear and agony of a five hour crisis. My doctor ordered complete bed rest for two days, after which the packing would be removed. If the bleeding resumed, a hysterectomy would be necessary. He said, "You need to know, the hospital has informed me they will get a court order to override your decision and give you a blood transfusion if it becomes necessary, so don't say another word about it. My hands are tied—they won't let a new mother die." He walked out of my room, his shoulders sagging visibly beneath his white medical jacket, possibly more disheartened than I was about the prospect, as he'd always promised to honor and respect my religious wishes. Lyman G. Armstrong, M.D. was one of the good guys in medicine. Secretly, I was relieved they'd taken the decision out of my control. I'd done my duty and could do no more, and no one would blame me for what might happen next.

There I lay, in my original labor room down the hall from where Jordan had been born, close enough for an immediate surgical procedure, if needed. I.V. drips pumped fluids and antibiotics into me. Once my catheter was removed, I'd call for assistance about once every hour to help me to the bathroom. Sound sleep was nonexistent. I prayed for the next two days and nights. Prayer was the normal response under those circumstances, but I'd become aware of another question I'd never thought about until then. "I was wondering if you'd really expect me to refuse a blood transfusion knowing I'd leave my three sons behind without a mother?" He didn't answer me, but I kept praying for confirmation that I'd done the right thing, the *only* thing I could've done—to refuse a blood transfusion. I'd always considered it a sure thing that I'd refuse a transfusion in an emergency, but that was for an *imagined* situation. This was real, and I did not want to die, even though I wanted to be faithful to Jehovah. But, was the Organization's explanation of the scriptures accurate? Did I actually refuse a life-saving blood transfusion, and did I *really* have to? In the back of my mind, after twenty years in The Truth, doubts slipped in. I was already a hero back at the Woodlawn Hall.

News travels fast. I felt guilty though, and couldn't shake it. I resented the decision I'd had to make.

In my private room on the Obstetric floor for the final two days, hospital personnel drifted in occasionally, saying they wanted to see the "miracle woman" they'd heard about. Apparently the news was all over the hospital—the woman whose God had performed a miracle. *So . . . I thought, maybe Jehovah did answer my prayers after all and kept me alive for three reasons—my sons.*

All the sordid details filtered in after Jordan and I left the hospital five days later. Mom had waited with Jesse and Jason in a private room, and Doctor Armstrong had come in often to keep them informed. Once, he sat on the couch with Mom and didn't say anything. Finally, he told them I'd be going back to surgery and to "Just pray—that's the only hope there is." Mom, Jesse and Jason closed their eyes and remained silent until they heard the results: their mother was alive.

I'd been lucky, and no I don't mean fortunate. *I mean downright lucky.* Once I arrived home, Barbara, Jerry's wife, came to stay for a week, and since Mom lived upstairs, I had two full-time helpers. They took care of the baby's needs. I didn't give him his first bath, or dress him, and I was too weak to breastfeed him adequately. I'd been given iron shots in the hospital which turned my rear-end black, not a pretty sight, and the skin on my face a putrid yellow. I forced myself to eat spinach at every meal and took iron pills for six months to build up my red blood cells.

Emma brought baby Anthony over to show him off. She encouraged me to keep on working to stay healthy so we could go out and have fun like the old days. Friends from Woodlawn dropped by almost daily to see the baby, and me—the brave new mother who'd done the right thing in the face of adversity. They looked at me differently now, as though I wore a halo.

The following month, my skin color returned to normal (on both ends) and I had enough strength to take care of my household by myself, for the most part. But during the first week, while lying in bed during the day, alone, hearing my baby's gurgles and cries and listening to Mom and Barbara going about their chores, I imagined what it would have been like in the house without me. Oddly enough, I felt as though I'd died and could visualize from a higher plane how life would've gone on for the others, as though I'd attended my own funeral. The baby's gurgles and household noises would have been the same, without me there to hear them. *How sad, I thought. I would've lost out on so much.*

I mourned myself; I missed me.

CHAPTER THIRTY-FOUR
NEW MOTHERS

Mall shoppers did double-takes when noticing our baby carriages as Emma and I strolled along. Our sons looked nothing alike—only their strollers were identical. One woman asked if our babies were twins. We couldn't wait for her to walk away to laugh at her.

We took turns watching the boys as we tried on jeans that didn't fit. The local health club offered a New Year's special, two for one. I bought the membership and shared it with Emma. Finally, our pelvic bones slipped back into place and we were our old selves, going out in service with my mom and Lydia, antique shops, Mexican restaurants, and occasionally hosting a ladies' luncheon in our own homes. Lydia once made the most fantastic seafood chowder I'd ever eaten and followed it with Red Cherry Sabayon, an orange custard pudding made with Grand Marnier liquor with tart cherries and whipped cream on top. On another occasion, she served Cherries Jubilee for dessert. It was the first time I'd ever seen anyone set fire to food on purpose. I loved it!

Jordan and Anthony grew from infants to toddlers to little boys. Within those three years, my mother developed a serious heart valve problem, preventing her from climbing stairs without difficulty, and yet her apartment was reached via a tall flight of outside steps in the rear of our home. For that reason, Jim and I decided it was a good time to fulfill our desire to move into the country a few miles across the Ohio River to Indiana, and we bought an eleven-acre farm with a creek and a barn with an ancient Massey-Ferguson tractor inside that Jim couldn't live without. The property had been developed with various fruit trees—over two-hundred apple trees alone, as well as a grape arbor and a sizeable strawberry patch. The previous owner had also kept honey bees and he taught Jim to manage them. We had the advantage of a walk-out basement/garage which we converted into a lovely apartment for Mom and Enos.

In the meantime, the famous heart surgeon in Louisville, Allan Lansing, performed an open-heart procedure on my mother. Dr. Lansing was one of the first surgeons to perform open-heart surgery in Louisville without blood transfusions and the word spread fast among Jehovah's Witnesses. Dr. Lansing didn't make a practice of transfusing blood on any of his patients, no matter their religious beliefs, as he felt the healing process was more successful without it. On the day of my mother's surgery, reporters and cameramen from *The Courier-Journal* newspaper were on site to feature Lansing's technique, and Enos found a smiling image of himself in *The Sunday Magazine* insert, a few days later, shaking hands with Dr. Lansing after Mom's surgery. Dr. Lansing had replaced her defective valve, solving Mom's problem of climbing steps. But we'd already moved, so there we were—in a new congregation with new friends.

Emma and I didn't see each other nearly as much since we weren't in the same congregation but we met frequently, sometimes at the ballet or the Louisville Orchestra, and most often spending time together with our little boys who were nearly six years old by then. We also kept in touch with regular phone conversations, and she relished filling me in on all the gossip from my old Woodlawn hall—who was pregnant, married and divorced, disfellowshipped or reinstated. Once she called me, saying, "Guess who's pregnant?" I guessed everyone I could think of, but to no avail.

Finally she said, "You goofball . . . it's ME!"

PART Three

CHAPTER THIRTY-FIVE
DOOM, DESPAIR, AND AGONY ON ME

"I don't entirely approve of some of the things I have done, or am, or have been. But I'm me. God knows, I'm me." ~ Elizabeth Taylor

Emma's baby Joey was born during the summer of 1989. The previous two years were the most tumultuous of my life, and the following two were like a rollercoaster ride gone bad! Let's start with the previous two years: Jim had been in and out of The Truth so many times, I'd lost count, devoting most of his quality time to his rapidly growing business.

Our move into the country had not produced the happy family results we'd hoped for. An industrious workaholic, Jim tended three gardens every spring and summer weekend and came inside only after dark with loads of fresh vegetables for me to can the next day. Sometimes I left the green beans to rot, tossing them into the trash bin because I didn't like green beans, didn't want to can green beans, and didn't respond well to being ordered around. He worked Jesse and Jason in the gardens, demanding, like hired help. "If you were my employees, I'd fire you," he'd said at one time, and I realized he actually viewed the four of us as people who worked for him. I had to make an appointment to discuss anything important with him.

Where had time gone? Jesse and Jason were going through the typical hormonal trauma teenagers often experience. Jordan would soon be heading to Kindergarten—I was losing my baby!

I discovered Jesse's runaway plan on the afternoon of his fifteenth birthday only after he failed to get off the school bus. The parent of one of his schoolmates called saying Jesse had told her daughter on the way to school about his strategy, but she didn't think he was serious. He hadn't been in class, and when he didn't ride the bus home, she figured he'd really gone and done it. The girl told her mother.

I called the police, and then Jim to let him know what was happening. He immediately headed for a bar with his business partner. That pissed me off because I'd expected him to come home to be with me. I needed him for support. The police searched for three hours and found Jesse seventy miles away, walking in the pouring rain beside a busy highway. The officers were much more sympathetic and compassionate than my own husband.

Around six o'clock in the evening, once the officers informed me they'd found Jesse, I called Jim, still at the bar, drunk. Jim said he wouldn't be home anytime soon and that we'd just leave our son in jail overnight to teach him a lesson. I didn't think it was legal to leave one's 15-year-old son in jail overnight for that reason, but it was closer and closer to the beginning of the end of our marriage. I knew Jesse had run away from Jim, not from home, but still I wanted him to be with us. Apparently, Jim had forgotten what it feels like to be fifteen. We'd had numerous phone conversations where he'd told me he couldn't wait to leave home because his father was a tyrant in the mornings, complaining and yelling at his mother, waking all the children with his anger.

With my mother in the passenger seat, I drove for over an hour in a heavy thunderstorm to bring Jesse home. Jim gave him a lecture and sent him to bed.

I waited anxiously every weekday after that until Jesse safely stepped off the school bus and walked down our driveway.

The following month, Jason had found himself in the middle of a knife fight and was injured by someone else's poor aim. He was to be suspended for the remainder of the school year. I made an appointment to appeal before the School Board, and I used several copies of the *Watchtower* and *Awake!* magazines to develop Jason's case. It was as easy as preparing a five-minute talk for the Ministry School. I acknowledged how awful the behavior of young people had become in the school system, blaming poor parenting and peer pressure. I stated that Jason was being raised in a Christian home that did not condone such behavior, summarizing by removing Jason from blame: Jason had been in the wrong place at the wrong time. I looked into the eyes of the men seated around the table with us, and I could see my efforts had been a waste of my time. Their minds had been made up already; the appeal was a farce. I considered the possibility that Jason had not told me the real story, that I'd just made a complete motherly fool of myself. The Board allowed him to finish the school year in summer school rather than repeat it in the fall, so I suppose my efforts weren't entirely in vain. Whether or not Jason appreciated what I'd done for him, I don't know. We lived fifteen miles from his school, and the busses didn't run during the summer semester. I drove him to class in the mornings and back home again each afternoon for six weeks—sixty miles a day for thirty days—eighteen hundred miles. I could've driven to a lovely beach in Florida instead. It occurred to me that being the mother of teenagers wasn't nearly as rewarding as when they were sweet little boys.

~*~

My life instantly changed on the first Sunday in August, 1988. Jim had taken the two older boys to cut grass at his place of business. Mom and Enos were out knocking on doors, as usual for a Sunday afternoon. Jordan and I had driven into New Albany, about fifteen miles from home, to shop for school supplies for his first day of Kindergarten, coming up within a couple of weeks. Later, when we were within a few miles of our home, police cars and fire trucks passed us with their sirens blaring. I saw black smoke rising high into the sky. We reached St. John's Road, but it was closed, jammed with emergency vehicles and dozens of curious bystanders. I inquired as to what was going on. The officer said a house was on fire down the road. I said, "I live down this road. Which house is it?" He described the house. *"That's MY house!"* He let me through the barricade and I pulled off into the grass across the road from our home.

I sat in the car, rolled the windows down, smelled the destruction of my life, watched the drama unfold, but it wasn't really me this was happening to. These things happen to other people. Then, I realized through all of the noises, the distress signals from emergency vehicles still on their way there, people shouting, etc., one of those siren-like sounds was Jordan crying. I scooted over and put my arms around him. I said, "Don't worry, honey. No one was at home and I'm sure Prince (our Collie) was outside. It'll be okay."

He continued to cry. I held him closer. Between sobs, Jordan said, "But . . . but my *toys!*"

The perfect solution immediately popped into my mind as a way to soothe my five-year-old. I knew our homeowners' insurance coverage would replace most of our contents.

"We'll buy you all new toys," I said.

He jumped up onto his knees. "OK! Now?"

"No, not right now, not today." I laughed at how this all sounded surreal, like watching a movie.

"When?" He was so excited to think new toys were to come out of the deal. I couldn't stop laughing. Some people cry during a tragedy. I guess I'm one who laughs uncontrollably. Finally, I calmed myself and we exited our car and walked down our long driveway toward the house, trying to stay out of the way of the firemen and water hoses. The house was gutted. Only brick walls and the bedroom wing remained.

Betty Crocker went up in flames, but she was replaceable. Jordan's baby book disappeared, but it was *not* replaceable. The majority of our family photographs weren't destroyed, although their edges were blackened.

Our insurance covered temporary housing. We located a small mobile home for sale and the owner allowed us to rent it. We had it delivered, pulled in alongside the ruins of our home, hooked into pre-existing utilities, and the five of us squeezed inside during the six months it took to rebuild. Mom and Enos moved temporarily into the home of friends.

While our house was being rebuilt, I had an enormous list of tasks to take care of each day, but I couldn't seem to think straight or remember important things. I sought mental health therapy, even though the Organization highly discouraged such worldly treatments. They counseled congregation members to stick close to Jehovah for peace of mind, which sent the message loud and clear that I had evidently failed to do so. I was prescribed Prozac for depression which enabled me to run around like a wind-up toy, accomplishing duties that would've made Superwoman proud.

The month after we moved into our new home, I couldn't remember one day from the next and was hospitalized for three weeks. A multitude of physiological tests showed no tumor or physical reason for memory loss. Finally, I was diagnosed with a medication-induced (Prozac) Bipolar Disorder and Attention Deficit Disorder. More medications were prescribed: Lithium to keep me down and Prozac to keep me up. Right in the middle is where I was supposed to be. I regained my focus and balance. My psychiatrist said I was suffering from Post Traumatic Stress Disorder and, in addition, gave me a book titled *Codependent No More*. I quickly absorbed the message from the book: I'd been making Jim's opinions and problems my own and trying to control the entire Universe!

While the manic episode was triggered by an anti-depressant, merely removing the drug from my system would not bring me back to normal. I was to struggle with Bipolar Disorder for the rest of my life—like Pre Menstrual Syndrome every day of each month—up, down, flat-lined, bouncing off walls, I never knew what mood I'd be in from one hour to the next.

The Organization held firm in their "suggestions" that a congregation member who drew close to Jehovah would not need psychotropic drugs and should not trust a psychiatrist or psychologist with their innermost feelings. Worldly physicians had no love of Jehovah and would possibly suggest that our religion might be part of our problem. In reality, it was feared that anyone with an emotional imbalance might put the Organization in a bad light. The Truth was touted as the answer to all problems.

I recently discovered that Bethel Headquarters had its own private pharmacy with shelves stocked full of Prozac, Lithium, and many other anti-depressant medications. Obviously, Bethel members with mental health issues were quietly allowed. Bethel maintained in-house JW mental health and medical teams to prescribe these drugs. Yet, back at home anyone who found it necessary to be under the care of a mental health professional was looked upon as spiritually weak. One three-year Bethel member I know sought treatment for depression and was told that her sadness was merely because she was a woman with cycles. Her issues were not addressed; three months later she attempted suicide. Fortunately, she lived to escape from the cult known as The Truth.

The friends from my congregation seemed to slowly back away from me. Those who ventured a conversation encouraged me to draw closer to God. "Rely on Jehovah," they'd say. "He will keep you safe during this time of trial." Emma's new baby kept her busy and didn't allow us much telephone time. Jim didn't seem to be interested in my health issues—they were *my* problem—he had his own concerns at work. My mother sympathized with me, but she also advised me to draw closer to Jehovah. Did no one have compassion for someone with a brain chemistry imbalance? I thought of my lifetime imaginary friend Dainy. She would understand, but I couldn't dare talk to myself; I'd feel crazier than ever!

Even though Jim's business kept him busy, he wasn't always emotionally absent. We occasionally had productive intimate conversations. In a rare moment of openness, Jim confessed that he likened our marriage to the lyrics of Judy Collins 1975 recording of "Send In The Clowns." I wondered if he thought he was the one who was "at last on the ground," while I was in "mid-air." Was he the one who "keeps tearing around," and I was the "one who can't move" or was it the other way around? I figured he applied this line to himself: "Just when I stop opening doors finally knowing the one that I wanted was yours, making my entrance again with my usual flair, sure of my lines, no one is there." He sensed he'd lost me long before I actually walked out the door.

I applied this line to myself: "I thought that you'd want what I want, sorry my dear." I'd always thought our religion was just as important to him as it was to me. I was mistaken.

I know better now, but at the time I was sure that everything was Jim's fault. We tried marital counseling for about six months. One day on the way home from a therapy session, he asked me if I knew why he often made fun of me.

"You've always done it but I have no idea why."

"Because I'm jealous of you—you make friends so easily, everyone likes you, but it's hard for me. So I do it to make myself feel better."

I pulled a throaty sound up from my stomach, and said, "*Really? That's it?*"

I guess he thought his explanation would satisfy me, make up for all of the disrespect he'd shown me over the years, but it backfired on him. What kind of man makes his wife feel bad so he can feel good? *A soon-to-be divorced man*, I thought. I could barely keep the rage I felt inside. I knew then I surely would lose my mind for good if I had to stay with him. I'd blamed him for so long for my unhappiness and, even though I realized my blaming Jim was part of the problem, I couldn't stop.

When I told Mom and Enos of my decision, Enos risked a smile, shook his head and said, "I never understood why you married him in the first place." I lightened up and laughed, hearing those words from the mouth of Jim's uncle. I filed for divorce and it was finalized on December 29, only eight months after our new home had been rebuilt.

Nagging advice from congregation members bombarded me. "Look around you—look at all you have. Why would you want to give this up?" What kind of friends are those who would've had me trade my happiness and peace of mind for material possessions and eleven acres of apple trees? "You won't be free to remarry if Jim hasn't committed adultery." Blah. Blah. Did they think I hadn't already thought this through? They didn't fool me—this was their way of meddling, trying to find out if he'd been unfaithful, which I didn't believe he had at the time. A different husband was the *last* thing on my list, but shutting them up was toward the top of it. How could I do that?

Jim assumed I was having an affair, otherwise I wouldn't want out of the marriage. To him, I was safely bought and paid for. I didn't think of it as an affair, but once I'd filed for divorce I considered myself free. So, yes, I had someone in my "back pocket" who was eager to be my rebound man, no strings attached. I affirmed Jim's suspicions and he wasted no time phoning an elder, for he would now be free to remarry, although I couldn't imagine who would want him. A quickie elder's meeting was held and I was disfellowshipped for adultery. I left the Kingdom Hall that night cold and emotionless with one exception: *Relieved.* Now the entire congregation *couldn't* talk to me. Check!

CHAPTER THIRTY-SIX
REBOUND MARRIAGES

Four months from the day of our divorce, Jim married his secretary. Surprise, surprise. Carolyn had suddenly taken an interest in *his* religion, and my mother was delighted to study the Bible with her. She was baptized in a hurry and they had a Jehovah's Witness marriage ceremony.

Hmmm. I wondered if their previous relationship, whatever it may have been, might explain my prior marital unhappiness, but it really didn't matter to me. My mother figured it *would* matter, and she made a point of telling me how confident she was that they hadn't been having an affair. "I truly don't care, Mom," I said. "I want Jim to be happy. He appears to be thrilled with his new wife, and I, on the other hand, am thrilled to be free, so we're both happy." Life is good.

Jim had asked for the house and acreage, so we split the equity of our property. I bought a log house on five acres a few miles away so the boys could stay in their schools and remain close to their dad and grandparents. Adjacent to the house was a huge, old white barn with cattle stalls, a massive loft and a red tin roof. I had grandiose dreams of converting it someday to a Bed and Breakfast.

When Jordan, then six, heard that his father was engaged, he wept. The wedding was to be held in our newly rebuilt home and Jordan was determined to stay away from the affair. "I'm *not* going!"

"Dad will be very unhappy if you don't go."

"I don't care. He makes *me* unhappy and I want him to marry you, not her."

"I'm sorry, son. I realize this doesn't feel good, but Dad's mind is made up. He loves Carolyn, not me."

Jesse and Jason, then sixteen and fourteen, tried everything they could think of to talk him into it, but Jordan was adamant.

His Kingdom Hall meeting attire consisted of a dark blue suit which he would soon outgrow. I went shopping a few days later and selected a new one along with a shirt and tie to match. The wedding was one week away.

"See? I bought you a new meeting suit," I said. "And, you can wear it to Dad's wedding in case you change your mind, or you can wear your other one. Or you can stay at home with me."

"I'm staying home with you." He stomped his foot.

"Okay. It's your choice; I'm not going to force you. Try this suit on so I can make sure it fits. If you're sure you're not going, you should let your dad know not to expect you."

He made a face as though he'd just eaten a nasty green vegetable, most likely canned asparagus. He tried his new suit on and studied his reflection in the mirror, changed back into his blue jeans, tossed the outfit onto his red Corvette water bed and ran outside to play in the barn.

I woke up early on Saturday, the morning of Jim's wedding, and thought about how happy he must be right now. Without any regard for misinterpretations or repercussions, I picked up the phone and called him. I wanted to tell him I was sincerely happy for him.

"Hi. I just called to tell you—."

"I have nothing to say to you," a robotic voice sounded back. He hung up.

I felt the sharp pain of an ice cold knife in my heart. *How odd*, I thought. I hadn't even warned him that Jordan might not be there.

Jesse and Jason were ready for the wedding around noon. Jordan sulked in front of the television. "Why don't you put on your new suit again and look in the mirror and think about going to the wedding?" I said.

Another asparagus face. But the next thing I knew, he had donned his *old* suit and was ready to go. I smiled at him, but he didn't return the expression. "You don't have to do this, you know," I said.

"Yes I do."

A few hours later they returned home and I noticed a hole in the knee of his trousers. According to the older boys, Jordan and his new step-brother had been playing in the yard, rolling down the grassy hills after the ceremony. I was glad I'd bought him a new suit for the meetings, and I didn't think anything more about it at the time.

Jesse dropped a bombshell in my lap. "Emma and Lydia catered Dad and Carolyn's reception. They served fancy tea sandwiches and quiche tarts, right there in the kitchen you designed!"

It wasn't the actual location of the wedding that gnawed at me. Knowing Jim, I trusted he'd offered them an overly generous amount of money, an offer they couldn't refuse, to send me a message that my friends weren't loyal since I was disfellowshipped. The message for me, however, was that Jim was mean-spirited and vindictive. He'd already instructed both our accountant and our insurance agent to discontinue business with me. (Did I mention Jim was mean-spirited?) Those two professionals were easily replaceable, but Emma was not. She was *my* friend. Jim could've afforded any expert caterer he wanted. He'd drawn a line in the sand, but why did

Emma go along with it? I needed to know.

On Monday, I dialed Emma's number.

"We shouldn't talk. I'm not supposed to."

"Right, I got that. Just give me one minute. Tell me why you went to Jim's wedding. Are you taking sides? Am I a total outcast, is that what this is?"

"No! You goofball. Mom and I looked at it like any other catering job, so yeah. Oh! It was kinda like a fairy tale inside your house. It's decorated just the way you left it." Emma giggled. "I expected you to round the corner at any time."

Very interesting. "Any *other* catering job? I didn't even realize you and Lydia were caterers. I'll just assume Jim was your first customer." Emma didn't respond. I rang off, telling Emma I'd talk to her later, if and when I was ever reinstated.

A few days passed and my mother came to my house to see her grandsons. As soon as I let her in the door, she said, "I pray Jim doesn't do to his new wife what he did to you."

"What are you talking about?" I said.

"Well. . . ." She cleared her throat and deeply inhaled. "You know how lax he was as the spiritual head of the house. I want him to walk the straight and narrow so Carolyn's spirit won't be dampened."

I rolled my eyes. "Don't hold your breath."

I had so much more to add, but I didn't because we weren't supposed to be conversing about spiritual matters. My mother bent the rules because that's the kind of mother she was, always on my side no matter what. I planned to keep it that way. I clearly understood Mom's vested interest in Carolyn's spiritual health since she'd studied the Bible with her, but I experienced a fleeting moment of jealousy to think that Carolyn would be my mother's new "Golden Child" since Mom couldn't *officially* associate with me. I knew I'd brought the "shunning" situation upon myself, and I was prepared to jump through those hoops to put everything back to normal. Jim swiped my insurance agent and my CPA in one fell swoop. He might even take Emma away from me, and Carolyn could take my place with Jim, good luck with that and more power to her, but she would *not* take my place with my mother!

~*~

I was at my sexual peak at forty-two, something I hadn't realized until after I divorced Jim who, though exhausted from work or gardening, never left me alone long enough for me to know what my own needs actually were! Since I was disfellowshipped, I no longer felt an obligation to limit myself to sex only within marriage. Like being on a merry-go-round, I tried the white rabbit, the carriage, and the gold pony. The ride was nice, but it went around and around, never arriving at a specific destination.

I think of that as the year of my mid-life crisis; I had so much fun I've often considered having another one. Finally, I took a weekend cruise with a girlfriend. We sat at a large round dining table for eight. When the twenty-five year old waiter put the moves on me, I thought, *why not?* I knew I'd never see him again, but when I arrived home, there was a card postmarked from Miami. *Coffee, Tea or Me*, it read on the front. Inside, he'd hand-written a note saying the short time we'd spent together meant more to him than I would ever know.

Damn! *Really?* Here I'd only wanted to see what a one-night stand was like. I knew I'd better hop off this ride before someone got hurt, specifically me! That's when Alan came into the picture.

Alan had a furniture-moving business; he'd moved us out of the house after the divorce. He had achieved two years' sobriety, and we talked a lot about alcoholism which helped me understand my dad's experience with addiction. Alan came in a compact package, much to my liking, and he had a great sense of humor—a laugh that always made me smile. I took an immediate liking to him and I did that rebound thing women often do. I asked Alan to marry me.

CHAPTER THIRTY-SEVEN
I WANT MY MOTHER BACK!

The thing was, truth be told (and this *is* about the truth, after all), I was miserable as a disfellowshipped person for several reasons. There were a lot of things I hadn't figured on. I hadn't realized how lonely I would be without my weekly phone conversations with Emma, and I hadn't thought out how difficult it would be for Mom. I couldn't ignore the sadness in her eyes, sadness I had caused and would have promptly removed in a short period of time. How devastated she must have felt to sit through the announcement at the Kingdom Hall on the night I was disfellowshipped. It must've felt like she'd lost her only child in death. I'd never once considered her feelings, only my own.

Jim and Carolyn lived in our rebuilt home, and Mom and Enos had moved back into their downstairs apartment which had been restored after the fire even more beautifully than before. The only time I saw or spoke to Mom was when I dropped off the boys or she came by to pick them up. It was dreadfully painful not being able to talk to her intimately as we'd always done, and I could tell she was equally as miserable, if not more. She didn't want to shun me, but she was under orders. She would bend the rules only so far. It's been said that guilt is the gift that keeps on giving. I couldn't go one day without that rotten feeling in my gut. I sometimes felt so depressed I could barely stand myself, and I'd dial Emma's number. When she answered I'd say the first thing that came to my mind, "I'm sorry, but I can't live through this without hearing your voice." She would remind me that she'd be in trouble if anyone knew we were talking, so *please* get reinstated as quickly as possible. But she never refused to talk to me for a couple of minutes. If I felt about to suffocate, talking with Emma infused me with just enough oxygen to keep me plugging along.

I figured I could be reinstated without much effort, simply haul myself back to the meetings regularly and everything would go back to the way it had been. But I wanted to remarry first because I didn't want to take a chance trying to find a JW husband. The candidates in my age group had already been picked over and rejected, for good reason.

So, Alan it was! We gave ourselves three weeks to plan the wedding. Alan bought the first suit he'd ever owned and I found a gorgeous black lace party dress on sale. I didn't believe in omens, but a black wedding dress was probably an omen if there ever was one. Jordan insisted I rent a tuxedo for him, and he was truly the cutest one there with his little red bow tie, cummerbund, shiny black dress shoes and his curly brown hair. A local judge drove out to the house early one Saturday morning to perform the wedding, attended by a handful of new friends I'd collected, and my cousins from Indianapolis who helped me throw a celebratory champagne brunch afterward.

The day before, I was stunned when Mom *and* Enos showed up at my door holding two large, living houseplants. We placed the greenery on the hearth of my creek-stone fireplace, where the wedding was to take place. Enos looked curiously around the log house, and I realized he'd never seen it before. Mom had always come to visit her grandsons alone, whereas Enos spent time with them on the weekends when they were at Jim and Carolyn's home.

My mother and I held each other and cried. They would not be at my wedding. My cousins were baffled at this and wanted to know why. I attempted to explain JW rules of disfellowshipping and shunning, but even then, their confused looks displayed the fact that they did not agree with this inhumane thing called shunning. They encouraged me to do whatever I had to do to find my way back to their beloved Aunt Gretchen.

Within two weeks, I was hospitalized for six days with double pneumonia and pleurisy. Mom came to visit each day and brought one or another of my sons with her. When I was released and well, she told me that she'd feared I would die while I was disfellowshipped. What kind of a funeral does a disfellowshipped person receive? It is not a pretty sight if a prior Witness dies while out of God's favor. Mom did the what-ifs in her mind, and she prayed for me, even though a JW is *never* to pray for a disfellowshipped person. But, she knew Jehovah could see into her pure heart, and into mine, so she wasn't worried about my resurrection. She wanted me to stick around for a long time!

~*~

The following year, Jim sold the house and moved into an adjoining county, taking the Massey-Ferguson tractor with him. Mom and Enos started looking for a place of their own. My log house had proved to be a much larger financial burden than I'd planned on. I sold it and built a modest home on two wooded acres and had an above-ground swimming pool erected right off the back deck. Mom and Enos bought two adjacent acres. We were neighbors once again!

Disfellowshipped for a total of twenty-two months, my mother and Emma were the only two JWs I'd talked to. When they disfellowshipped me, the committee of three elders told me I would not be allowed to share anything scripturally with my children, as their father was a baptized brother and that would be his responsibility. *Well, good luck with that*, I thought. I was not even allowed to pray at meals out loud with my three sons at mealtime. Jesse and Jason weren't interested in prayer, so we had a moment of silence. I was startled one time when Jordan spoke up, giving thanks. His brothers laughed at him, so he said "amen" and never attempted it again.

Since I could not, and Jim never found the time or interest, Mom studied the Bible every week with Jordan. He was a question-asker just like I had been at such a young age. One day he came to me, perplexed. He'd asked his grandmother how she knew the Bible was from God. "Because the Bible says so," was her answer.

A disfellowshipped sinner will always qualify for salvation and forgiveness, followed by reinstatement into the congregation, unless he committed the *unforgivable* sin. It was never clear what that was, exactly, but it had something to do with grieving the Holy Spirit. The Organization's explanation of the unforgivable sin wavered continuously. At first they said Sodomites, destroyed in Lot's day, would not be resurrected into Paradise because they had grieved the Holy Spirit. Jehovah had destroyed them once, so it would be fruitless to bring them back just to kill them off. Then, new light was shed on the subject. You see, Jehovah had this super-duper flashlight, kind of like a laser beam, I'd imagined, and he'd shine it down on the Organization so they could see The Truth more clearly. If the batteries were weak, the light was dim, and so they waited for new light. In any case, this particular case of fresh battery injection indicated that the Sodomites had been destroyed *before* Jesus came to save us all, so they would have a second chance. Good for them, I thought.

A few years later, they altered their position again!

Who cared? I wondered. By this time, I'd grown weary of habitual adjustments to scriptural interpretations, especially those not applicable to modern day life. Weren't they wasting their time trying to pinpoint what Jehovah would do in the future? If the Sodomites were to be resurrected, then that's where they'd be. Leave it up to God and see what He decides. Let the future unfold as it may. Of course, Sodomites would undoubtedly have to change their ways, but they'd be in Paradise if Jehovah saw fit.

~*~

During my committee meeting with three elders where it would be determined if I was repentant enough to be reinstated, an aggressive, former-Marine elder fixated on one irrelevant thing. He didn't seem to care about the past, or anything but my middle son Jason, whose hair was down to his shoulders. "What are you going to do about Jason's hair?"

I blinked and frowned. "What about Jason's hair?"

"It's as long as a girl's! The Bible says that is a sin," he said. "Why did you allow this?"

I felt as though I'd been invited to a public argument, and while I knew it wasn't necessary to attend, bile immediately formed in my throat. I jumped right in. "As I recall, you were the very one who informed me I was not to give scriptural council to, or pray with, my sons during the nearly two years when I was on the outside looking in. Furthermore, Jason is baptized, so you as an elder had the responsibility to look after him, especially if you saw him committing a sin." I paused for effect, then added, "I never noticed you in our driveway offering to take them to the meetings."

"That was Jim's responsibility," he said. *Well, pass the buck,* I thought.

"Jim studied with them until he remarried and then went on about his merry life with his new wife and step-son." The two older boys were slippery and had lost all interest in The Truth. Jim couldn't pin them down for a family study, so he'd followed his old method of operation—he gave up.

I continued my tirade, in a polite but firm tone of voice. "You lived right down the road, but never once stopped by to see my sons." Then, ignoring my original intention to restore my relationship with my mother, I threw it all into the wind. "Anyway, I don't understand why we're on the subject of Jason's hair. It's not the issue here. Why don't you ask me if I'm having sex with someone other than my husband? That's why you disfellowshipped me in the first place."

The room became abnormally quiet for a moment.

"I'm sure if you were still misbehaving you wouldn't want reinstatement into Jehovah's Christian congregation," he said in a superior tone. Then he crossed his legs and folded his arms, staring me down.

I smiled, looking him straight in the eye. The subject was dropped.

Later that evening, Brother Graham called me to inform me the elders had prayerfully made the decision to reinstate me.

"Really?" I said. "You're going to let this loud mouth back in?"

"Of course. How could we not? By the way, I was proud of you, the way you stood up for yourself." He chuckled. "You've always been one of my favorite people. I trust you can make this commitment to Jehovah work. I'll help you any way I can." Brother Graham became my go-to elder from then on.

The announcement of my reinstatement was to be made at the Kingdom Hall the following Tuesday, on the evening of what would've been mine and Jim's twenty-fifth anniversary, July 2, 1991. When I realized what the date was, I hoped if Jim realized it too, he wouldn't feel sad because of the coincidence. Jason, furious that his hair had come into question, asked a friend to shave his head, leaving one long clump hanging down the back. "We'll see what they think about my hair now," Jason said. I wouldn't allow him to go with me that evening, as it would attract way too much attention and I'd be a nervous wreck even more than I was.

A crowd gathered around Alan and me after the announcement. They sized him up, thinking that soon enough he would become a Jehovah's Witness, too.

The very next day Emma brought Anthony and Joey over, and while the boys played in the pool, she brought me up-to-date on the past two year's worth of gossip. She got a kick out of Jason's new hair style, as I sat there shaking my head. We touched on the subject of Jim's wedding, and Emma said, "Jim told me about your phone call that morning. You actually told him you wanted him back?"

"I did *what?* No! I called to tell him I was happy for him, but he hung up on me. I didn't want him back. Jordan was the one who wanted that—not me."

"In his dreams," Emma said with a giggle.

I kicked myself for fearing Jim would be sad about my reinstatement announcement on our twenty-fifth wedding anniversary. What a fool I was to think he would even think about it. However, in the back of my heart I never stopped caring about Jim's feelings.

Emma and I developed a routine from then on. The boys would splash us from the pool as we sat under the umbrella on the deck with our Coconut Chews, or Emma's favorite—Lemon Squares. A poolside margarita always went well with dessert bars. My mother and Enos would walk over to visit Emma and her children. The new Betty Crocker Cookbook didn't have the identical recipes as the original—the Coconut Chews recipe was gone! Emma to the rescue—she'd copied it from my old cookbook. I have that very same recipe in her handwriting, and ever-so-often I make them out of respect for the memory of Emma and our good times out by the pool with our children.

~*~

117

The following year, I heard the bad news on the telephone; Emma had become seriously ill during the night and was at Jewish Hospital in Louisville, undergoing surgery. I went straight across the bridge only to hear the dreaded diagnosis of the ugly cantaloupe sized tumor—yes it was cancer after all.

CHAPTER THIRTY-EIGHT
MARGARITAS AND BLUE EYE SHADOW

Emma's doctors gave her eighteen months to live at the most, with aggressive chemotherapy treatment that would leave her bald, sick and weak. She opted instead for a strict cancer-killing diet, homeopathic and alternative medications. The friends from the Woodlawn Hall pulled together and took up generous collections, allowing Emma and Lydia to make several trips to Mexico for medicine and treatments. She soaked her feet in exotic liquids to extract toxins and her feet became purple-stained. But she was very much alive and finally she was cured! She'd gone over three years cancer-free, twice as long as the medical doctors had predicted.

Tequila wasn't on her anti-cancer diet, but occasionally she begged me to meet her at Chi-Chi's for a chimichanga, chips with salsa and a frozen margarita. She'd lean across the table and say, "Don't tell anybody." She whispered it as though everyone else in the restaurant knew she was cheating on her diet.

"Well . . . you have to live, too," I said, but I wondered if I was enabling her to renege on her healthy eating plan.

"Once or twice a year can't do me any harm, do you think?" She looked at me as though I had all the answers. I shrugged and told her she probably knew more than I would. "What's really harmful," she said, "is what we do to our bodies with make-up. Do you know that blue eye shadow is the worst?" She glared at me for the longest time, until I finally understood.

I was wearing blue eye shadow.

"Oh, great," I said.

She studied me with a familiar expression, like when she'd told me I was wearing too much blush that day years before.

I make sure, now that I am aware of the dangers, to use natural, non-toxic products, but when I apply blue eye shadow, I think of Emma's emerald eyes and the look on her face when she innocently explained how eye make-up infuses itself into the delicate tissue of the eyelid and goes straight for the blood stream.

CHAPTER THIRTY-NINE
CANCER IS A BITCH

"Think for yourselves and let others enjoy the privilege to do so, too." ~Voltaire 1694-1778

Alan and I went on a Florida vacation where I bought Emma and myself matching gold charm bracelets right after her cancer diagnosis. I added identical charms each time I took a trip after that. Emma brought back coins from Mexico, and we had them attached to our bracelets. She bought the letter "J" and I bought the letter "E". Whenever we were together, we always wore our matching bracelets. Emma would laugh and say, "We're so *charm*ing when we're together."

Alan and I didn't last long. I'd wisely held on to my worldly friends, and the very young daughter of one couple asked, "What happened to Alan?" I smiled at her innocent expression and told her the marriage just didn't work out. She nodded as though she understood, but I knew she didn't. I barely understood myself. But what had I expected? I'd barely taken the time to really get to know Alan in the first place. When I brought up the subject of divorce, he said he didn't want one.

"How could you not? Surely you can see we're not happy."

His next remark led me to a quick decision. "I know, but I like the house and the pool."

"You've *got* to be kidding me," I said.

"No, I'm serious. I'm comfortable here."

With that, my feelings for him faded to total black. Alan's honesty put the final nail on the coffin with our marriage locked inside. I figured, considering the hell I'd gone through to achieve my first divorce, I wasn't going to waste any more time on this empty relationship. We divorced after two years; Alan was a super nice guy, but he no longer lived in the woods in a house with a pool, thanks to the prenuptial agreement I'd insisted he sign a week before our wedding. I sighed with relief and gave myself credit for at least thinking that one through.

If I had owned a butt-kicking machine, I would've stood next to it several times a day. A non-JW girlfriend suggested I think of it, not as a marriage and divorce, but as a legal affair. "After all," she said, "it only lasted two years."

"If only I'd been in a position to have an affair," I lamented. "But, as a Jehovah's Witness, marriage was the only option for me. So now I suffer the humiliation of being twice divorced."

"Two isn't bad. Nobody's counting but you, so get over it," she said.

But had I learned my lesson? No, I had not. I turned around and did that rebound thing *again*! And for the same reason as before. Alan had moved into an apartment with one of his employees, and while I didn't believe it was a sexual relationship, it had the appearance of one. I was told by an elder that I was now scripturally free to remarry, but *only in the Lord*— a welcome proclamation of freedom from the Organization that governed my every move.

I dated Ken five months longer than I cared to remain celibate. We'd met at work where I was a mental-health transcriptionist and he was a social worker, specializing in crisis counseling. The congregation members hadn't thought too poorly of my marriage to Alan since that had happened while I was *out of The Truth.* But they treated me differently after husband number three. Marrying an unbeliever is frowned upon in the Organization, and they pried my Mom with masked, trivial questions as to why I would do such an *un-Christian* thing. Their meddling provoked her, as she didn't want to reveal any of the private details to anyone, knowing there would be gossip galore at the Kingdom Hall which would stir up a real mess, according to Enos, whose description of a *mess* was "five pounds of shit in a three-pound bag!"

~*~

Three years after Emma's original tumor, my mother was diagnosed with colon cancer in April, 1995. She had emergency surgery and was fitted with a temporary colostomy. I pleaded with her to try Emma's method of treatment because . . . it had worked! But Enos wanted her to have immediate chemotherapy and she tended to agree with him. She was eighty years old. During her eight months of chemotherapy, I'd walk over from my house next door to spend Tuesday and Thursday meeting nights and Sunday mornings with her. We listened to the program from a speakerphone connected at the local Kingdom Hall, so Enos could attend the meetings in person and spend time with his spiritual brothers and sisters. Mom and I knew he needed and would benefit from the encouragement.

During that period, I never missed a meeting via speakerphone, but no longer went in the ministry work. I stayed with my mother so Enos could go out—that was my excuse. In reality, I was reticent to recommend the Organization to others since I had serious doubts about it myself—no longer confident that it was The Truth. So much label-making going on, so much gossip, and so much hypocrisy. Why would Jehovah allow chaos in His organization? Jehovah's people no longer seemed to be the *happy people* from the past. When I analyzed my feelings, the words, *I'm tired . . . tired . . . just plain tuckered out,* came to mind.

The world hadn't ended in 1975 as predicted and thousands of people had left the Organization, having come to think of it as a false prophet. Those deserters were labeled as apostates and mentally diseased naysayers, and we were warned not to pay any attention to their words. While the Organization admitted that Armageddon was seriously overdue, they had the answers for that, as well as answers for everything else. Like the game of Jeopardy on television, it was your job to ask the questions. Have a question? Bingo! Here's the answer. So easy you don't even have to think for yourself. They even had a section in the back of the *Watchtower* magazine titled *Questions From Readers*. Questions about scriptures and their meaning for us today. Who is this supposed to represent? Which dragon in the Book of Revelation is the red one? What about the white horse? And which one breathes fire and what does that mean, really? On and on and on. The answers all made sense to me. Well, almost all of them. There was one in particular that seriously bothered me a lot and I never came to grips with the Organization's explanation. But, to doubt their heaven-sent enlightenment was to doubt Jehovah, and so I kept it tucked in the back of my mind.

During my mother's recovery, Brother Graham stopped by to visit. I had just delivered Mom and Enos' lunch and evening meals, as I did every day. As I walked back to my house, Graham called out to me as an afterthought, "It would certainly be good if you could come back to the Kingdom Hall soon. You'd benefit from the uplifting spiritual association in view of the fact your mother is ill." I smiled and waved from across the yard, thinking to myself, *you pious, self-righteous bastard. Where do you think I am when Enos is at the meetings and out in service? Do you assume he merely waltzes off and leaves his wife by herself?*

Why do people make judgments on perception alone, rather than do a little fact-finding research? He hadn't seen me at the meetings, thus I must not have been there, right? Rage simmered underneath my skin and my body temperature elevated a degree or two. I picked up the telephone later that afternoon and tactfully set him straight. "I prepare fourteen meals each week for my mom and step-dad; I listen to all of the meetings with my mother at her home; I work three days a week as a bookkeeper in Louisville as well as manage my immediate family's needs." Jordan was going on thirteen; Jesse was twenty-three and still living at home. To say my plate was full was an apt description of my life. Most nights I was drained, exhausted long before it was time to go to bed. Brother Graham humbly apologized and said he hadn't been thinking straight. *No shit, Sherlock,* I thought. I doubted I was still one of his favorite people.

Throughout my mother's illness, we spent many hours together, quality time. She said she couldn't imagine her life without me. We'd had dozens of adventures with the kids, and sometimes with Jim, too. Opryland, Disney World, a cruise on the SS Norway to the Caribbean with our very own balcony! Kings Island in Cincinnati, the beaches on both coasts of Florida, shopping malls and movie theaters. She confessed that she never really did "get" Star Wars, but not to tell Jesse and Jason such a thing. She assured me she wouldn't have had nearly as much fun if I hadn't come up with those ideas, and she always went along with them. She considered me her social secretary.

Our conversations included a discussion of my doubts and Mom's, as well. What a surprise to realize my mother had doubts! She admitted several issues which caused her misgivings, and other situations she'd been aware of when hypocrisy was difficult to ignore. She said that at one time she had even considered *leaving* the Organization. This had come about two years previous when I'd married Ken.

~*~

I thought I had my marriage runway cleared for takeoff. I'd called Brother Graham and told him my intention. I asked him if this would in any way conceivable cause me any problems with being disciplined by the congregation. Ken had told me he would like to study the Bible with an elder to learn more about my religion. Brother Graham said he'd enjoy a discussion with Ken, and for me not to worry. I was doing nothing wrong other than going against the scriptural advice to marry only in the lord. But that was not a disciplinary matter. It was one's own personal decision.

I asked my mother to be my matron of honor, but after some consideration she and Enos concluded that it wouldn't be setting a good example for the congregation members, especially in view of Enos' elder status, and they were both regular pioneers. So she declined and I asked my cousin, Tracey, instead. Soon, however, my mother had second thoughts, because the wedding was to be in Texas and she would not be there. Finally, Ken asked her to consider merely going along with us, not to participate in the ceremony, if that would help her make a decision she could live with. Near the last two weeks before we left, she decided she wanted to go. Enos told her to do whatever made her happy, and she bought her airfare. Ken and I were elated! During the week we were in Texas, when Enos was asked where Gretchen was, Enos merely said she was in Texas with Joanna and the boys. Enos was a man of few words. Up until then, no one realized I'd gone out West to get married for the third time.

We arrived back home on a Sunday, and I chose not to attend the meeting on Thursday night because Ken and I considered ourselves to be in "honeymoon mode" and went to dinner and a movie. The next morning I received a phone call from a friend who said, "They gave a talk about you last night." I laughed. "What did they say about me?" I thought this person was joking. The thirty-minute talk lambasted anyone in the Christian Congregation who would marry outside of The Truth, disobeying God's command to marry only in the Lord. The audience then heard the words that such a person could be "marked" which would mean others wouldn't want to socialize with her and could even go so far as to ignore this person at Kingdom Hall meetings if they felt speaking to such a person would damage their spirituality. I had been passive-aggressively, officially marked!

The next phone call was the one I made to Brother Graham. "Why did you tell me I wouldn't suffer any negative consequences from marrying Ken, and then tell the congregation to mark me?"

"Your name wasn't mentioned," he said.

"Oh, come on! Really, just tell me why?"

"Another sister, (name withheld), got married last week, too. We didn't want to see a trend starting."

This other "sister" was one who hadn't attended meetings for at least a year. Who would have even expected her to marry a witness? She was the daughter of one of the regular ones, though, so I suppose people would have heard about it. I went back to the Kingdom Hall the next week, fully expecting to be ignored. Many did, at first. Ken decided he no longer had any interest in discussing our beliefs with Brother Graham. I guess he marked Jehovah's Witnesses just as they had marked me, and I didn't blame him one bit. He attended a Christian church in Louisville, and he noted he'd never seen one genuine Christian treat another one so rudely. But that wasn't the end of it.

The brothers wasted no time calling a committee meeting with Enos and Mom. Those three pompous elders actually had the audacity to *scold* her for traveling to Texas with Ken and me and my sons for our wedding. They questioned Enos as to how he, as an elder, would *allow* his wife to be an accomplice to my behavior, marrying a worldly man.

Enos didn't get fired-up very often, but when he did, it was a sight to behold. "You might as well talk to your butt when your head hurts," Enos said. "It's nobody's business. You can remove me as an elder and a pioneer if you see fit, I can't control that, but you'll *never* stop me from serving Jehovah." The big boys backed off. There was no action they could take anyway, but the three amigos strutted out of that meeting—mission accomplished, according to my mother.

~*~

That craziness led my mother to consider leaving the Organization. When she told me about the meeting they'd called with her and Enos, I was surprised. She'd kept it to herself because she was one who responded patiently to bad situations rather than reacting haphazardly. I told her that if I'd known about it, I would've created an ugly scene and left the Organization with her. She probably had imagined that would be the outcome.

"So, why didn't you leave?" I inquired. We sat for a couple of minutes in silence before she answered.

"Where else would I go?"

When she said this, I knew exactly what she meant. I could think of no other place either. The Organization made it clear there was nowhere else to worship the one true God, Jehovah. There was nowhere else to go. *Nowhere.*

Jehovah's Witnesses don't use traditional religious music at their services. Their Kingdom Melodies songbook uses lyrics and notes composed only by Witnesses. One song in particular is sung often: Keep Your Eyes on the Prize. Witnesses are repeatedly admonished to always look straight ahead, never to the left or to the right; one should live his life, not for today, but for the future—finish the race for the grand prize. This is where the blinders come in handy. They restrict a horse's vision, placed as they are on either side of the eyes, to keep the animal focused on what is in front of him, so he'll pay attention to the race and not the crowds. The term "blinder" is also used metaphorically to refer to people with an overly narrow focus or inability to see the larger picture.

Two years after those meaningful conversations with Mom, when we'd agreed there was nowhere else to go, my blinders finally fell off. I became conscious of the fact that I didn't need to "go" anywhere else. Rather, I merely needed to stop *being* in a cult. I needed to *be* somewhere—with myself. By then, my mother had been gone for well over a year. I subconsciously waited until after my mother's death to make that quantum leap.

CHAPTER FORTY
ANOTHER TUMOR

Ken traveled every year to Texas to spend Christmas with his family. During that time in 1995, Jordan and I went to Chicago. I showed him The Field Museum, the Aquarium and the Lincoln and Sears Towers. At the Field Museum gift shop I bought two marble apple-shaped charms for Emma and me. Jordan and I returned to our hotel room where I discovered a voicemail message on my cell phone from Emma, crying hysterically, begging me to call her back as soon as possible.

"I have another mass in my abdomen," she wailed.

"Is it cancer?"

"The blood tests don't show it, but it's a growth of some kind. The doctors want to do exploratory surgery, but they can't operate because it's practically attached to the aorta."

Oh no. I knew what that meant. If the aortic artery was accidently punctured, the results would be fatal without a blood transfusion. Emma was surrounded by people who'd contributed lots of money to keeping her well, and they were fastidiously against blood transfusions. Emma had no choice but to go along with it, and I believe she wanted to because of her love of The Truth, but I, personally, had developed doubts as to if it was a necessary requirement. This woman stood a chance of losing her life and leaving behind two children and a husband if she didn't have that mass removed.

During the next two years, Emma tried every test and healing method available: CT scans, x-rays, MRI's, blood tests, alternative treatments, purple foot soaks and a healthy eating regimen. No more margaritas for us, not even one!

Alas! She discovered what she believed would be the ultimate solution. A clinic in New York specialized in laser techniques, and she was convinced they would be able to remove the mass without surgery. She would have her scans and films sent up to them for consultation and negotiation with her health insurance company to cover the medical charges.

In the meantime, the mass enlarged. Her blood tests were always negative for cancer, however, so Emma remained positive and upbeat about the prognosis, still refusing the doctor's requests to be allowed to administer a blood transfusion. *Only in an emergency,* the surgeons pleaded. But, for Jehovah's Witnesses, an emergency is no excuse. The Biblical law is clear, and if it is disobeyed, disfellowshipping with no chance of life in Paradise is your punishment.

I have since learned (recently, and on good authority) that there are brothers high in ranking order at the Society's Headquarters who've been allowed, encouraged even, to accept blood transfusions because their value to the Organization was of more importance than the blood prohibition. When I think of the value of a mother to her children, I am enraged at the hypocrisy of the men who make decisions affecting the lives of millions.

Cancer didn't kill Emma; religion did.

CHAPTER FORTY-ONE
SAYING GOODBYE TO MOM

Two months after that phone call from Emma about her newly discovered abdominal mass, my mother elected a surgical procedure to repair her colon. With cancer in remission she no longer required the nuisance of a colostomy; the bag burped and farted when and wherever it pleased. Sadly, she didn't recover from the effects of general anesthesia; she died from respiratory failure the third day after surgery.

In reality, chemotherapy is what took my mother's life. She'd been in surgery to remove the colostomy bag for six hours! This, due to the fact that chemotherapy treatments had fused her intestines, causing the surgeons to spend a dangerous amount of time trying to separate them while she was under an extended period of general anesthesia. If only she'd followed the holistic way of healing, she might have lived much longer.

I held her hand as she took her last breath, and when her nurse suggested her hearing would be the last to go, I talked incessantly, telling her exactly what she would want to hear. I assured her I would go to all of the meetings from now on, and I'd spend my days out in service with Enos. Not to worry, I'd be there waiting for her after the resurrection. I really meant those things when I said them. Finally, Enos patted my arm, pointing to Mom's heart monitor. She no longer had a heartbeat. I would have to wait to see her again in Paradise.

Enos and I decided on a full day's visitation and viewing at a local funeral home, with cremation to follow. I chose a delicate pink crepe blouse I'd bought for her the year before, and we selected a vibrant spray of tropical plants for her casket. Many of our friends ordered tropical plant arrangements: bird of Paradise, bougainvilleas, banana trees, palm fronds and orchids. Emma and Lydia sent a clear glass vase with white silk Calla Lilies which I still have to this day. The chapel resembled the Caribbean cruise that Mom, Jordan and I had enjoyed together.

We held a Memorial Service and one extra visitation day. I took some time with Enos and my sons to compose a portion of the service to remind those in attendance of the happy woman they'd all loved:

A favorite photo of Gretchen is one taken at the age of four, shortly after her parents had discovered that she had eaten a very large bowl of strawberries and then denied having done so. Gretchen explained that the berries tasted so good, having gone back for another and then another, thinking just one more wouldn't be missed. She, however, was literally caught red handed and decided to always tell the truth from then on.

As a mother, Gretchen felt it a privilege to have shared her life with one daughter, a relationship equally nurturing and enriching to both. They shared their feelings, joys and frustrations, developing an enduring friendship which weathered the heartaches and delights that accompany family life. To describe Gretchen, her daughter uses the word "patience". She never raised her voice, even when disciplining her as a child, but always got her point across. Gretchen recently reminded Joanna of the time when an imaginary friend was blamed for something Joanna did. Gretchen spanked them both—Joanna learned a valuable lesson since she got two spankings.

As a grandmother of three boys, she is described by them as "fun" and as always putting others' needs ahead of her own. They have numerous fond memories, and many videos, which was a hobby of Gretchen's, of trips to amusement parks, the ocean, museums, shopping for candy and toys, trips to the bowling alley—the list is unending. She was a "fun" grandmother, and once again never raised her voice when disciplining them. One grandson (Jason) fondly remembers her as a "softie" and boasts that she had trouble catching him with her ruler, and when she did it didn't hurt anyway.

As a wife, Enos describes her as perfect. Their marriage was comfortable and comforting to those close to them.

I spent the entire visitation day on my feet, chatting with everyone, making sure I didn't overlook any of her visitors, looking at my mother in her casket, touching her, and trying to absorb the fact that I'd actually lost her. So many people came by and some were from her distant past. No one seemed to have forgotten Gretchen, and, in fact, she was a truly unforgettable woman.

One couple in particular grabbed my undivided attention as they walked into the chapel—Bill and Jeannette Hastings—all the way from Indianapolis! Jeanette still had that orange-red braided knot on her head! I wondered how long her hair actually was by now. Close to ninety years old, they'd driven one-hundred miles to pay their last respects. Hearing their voices again brought a flood of memories and tears.

Emma arranged a babysitter for her children so she could spend the day with me. She stuck around, that girl did, although most of the time she spent in a cushioned chair, away from the crowd. Whenever I looked over toward her, we'd lock eyes and she'd send her love in a smile to let me know she was there for me. I'd never seen such dedication before—most people came, paid their respects, and left. Not Emma. Sometimes she was flat-out staring at me. I was curious as to what she was thinking and why she would want to stay from morning till late afternoon in a funeral home. Did she wonder what it might be like if she died, imagining how I would handle it? Would I stand near her casket and touch her too? Would I cry and put my arms around her mother or her children? Was she trying to comprehend how people would react to her death, as though she knew she didn't really have as good a chance as she'd let on about the successful laser surgery she'd planned? Was she looking over the crowd wondering which of those people might be at her own funeral? I'll never know, but my imagination runs wild.

CHAPTER FORTY-TWO
THE PHONE CONVERSATION IN QUESTION

Out of all the time I shared with Emma, in person and on the phone, probably some of our most intimate conversations were over the phone. The last six months of her life we spent mostly on the phone. I recall visiting her in person only twice in the hospital. She had good color and energy and was only in "for a few tests," she'd said. She'd kept me in the dark.

It was during one of those phone calls Emma shared a disturbing bit of information. She told me Thomas had the tendency to be rough with their boys when disciplining them. She explained he'd been abused by his step-father as a child, but she never elaborated what type of abuse it was. I didn't ask, but I found it hard to believe the mild-mannered Thomas I knew was capable of being mean to Anthony and Joey. Emma explained she always made sure to step in and calm him down when Thomas was "too rowdy" but I was never sure exactly what that meant. Again, I did not ask for details.

One cold February day, I was at work and my boss was out of the office. I called Emma from my cell phone to see how she was feeling. She was working on getting the funds for that trip to the New York clinic. They'd seen her x-rays and scans, and promised to use their techniques to break up and remove her mass without surgery. The insurance company's paperwork was delayed, but she was confident she would soon reach the end of her abdominal problem.

In that phone conversation, I told Emma about a mutual friend of ours who had recently been divorced and had taken a waitressing job. One of her customers asked her out on a date, and yet his wife had died only eight weeks before. Without thinking, I added, "Of course, his wife had been sick for a long time." I regretted those words as soon as they slipped from my mouth. Oh, how cruel that must have sounded to Emma.

She was quiet, and I held my breath, wondering if I should try to explain, or if that would cause me to dig myself in deeper than I was already.

She asked, "What do you think about men marrying on the rebound?"

"It happens." I said. "I mean, look at Enos: he wasn't widowed for an entire year when he married my mother. But, wait . . . are you thinking of Thomas and yourself? Because if you are, this procedure you're going to have is going to make you well. That's what you've always told me. I don't think you have to worry about it."

"Yes, I know. I'm not. But just in case I don't make it," she confided. "I made him promise never to remarry."

"Why on earth would you make him promise that?"

"If he married some chick on the rebound, who would be there to protect my boys?"

A long pause ensued while I absorbed her real meaning—her actual concern. "Oh . . . you're referring to what you told me about Thomas before?"

"Duh. Plus, how would you feel if your husband hooked up with somebody right after you died?"

The business line rang, and as I answered the company phone I heard my boss coming in the rear door. I had to think of something fast. He stopped off at the restroom before coming into my office. I rejoined Emma, assuring her that our situations weren't similar enough to compare. Jim was already married and the boys had resigned themselves to their step-mother, and besides I'd always wanted him to be happy no matter what. I told her if Ken wanted to remarry quickly, it was okay with me as long as he was happy. Then again, I wouldn't have Emma's problem, that of protecting my children.

"How can you be so casual about all of this?" Emma asked when I'd finished with my long-winded explanation.

My boss was heading up the hallway. "Look, I'll tell you what. You're not going to die, but if you do, I'll solve that problem: I'll marry Thomas myself and I'll protect your kids!"

"You goofball!" Emma giggled. We both knew I was kidding, grasping, trying to ease her mind, as impossible as it was. I was already married for one thing and old enough to be Thomas's mother on top of all that.

"I must go—let's talk about this later," I said.

Still deeply saddened by the loss of my mother, I refused to face the reality of the close proximity of Emma's death. I planned to find the right time to discuss the remarriage issue with her, but I would've had to *make* the time, and I never did. I regret that I didn't. She died six months later.

133

CHAPTER FORTY-THREE
GOODBYE EMMA

I received the phone call early on a Saturday morning, the day before Emma died. She was hospitalized, unconscious, and everyone anticipated today would be her last day. *What?* How could this be? What about the laser surgery in New York? She'd been there and they turned her away. When they saw how large the mass was, they told her there was nothing they could do now. It was too late—it was over. A little more time and she'd be resting permanently, waiting for Paradise.

I rushed to the hospital and nearly bumped into her father and Thomas as I stepped off the elevator. Thomas hugged me and we cried. Her father directed me toward Emma's room, but he warned me that I wasn't going to like what I was about to see. He was right. Emma lay flat and lifeless on her deathbed.

How did something like this happen? Thomas explained. When Emma heard the final decision at the clinic in New York, she'd wept and admitted to him that she'd been a fool, going all this time not allowing the doctors to remove it. He'd snuggled beside her and they'd lain there for a long time, sobbing together. He'd brought her home to her parents' house, and they explained to their children that she wasn't going to make it after all. She died within two weeks, and all that time I thought she was receiving treatment.

I'd assumed she was in New York; why hadn't she called me? "She had everyone fooled, even herself." Thomas said. They'd believed it would be the answer to their problems, and when Emma became conscious of the fact that she was dying, she was embarrassed she'd *allowed* it to happen. She couldn't face anyone, especially me, for some reason.

Her hospital room filled with members of the Woodlawn Congregation, and others—relatives and neighbors. Some stayed for a short time, others for the long haul, as I did. Congregation members hovered by her bedside and sang out loud, Kingdom Melodies about the resurrection into eternal life on Earth. Almost everyone joined in, but I didn't—it seemed hot and crowded, almost suffocating. Lydia remained down the hall in a private room. She refused to come in with the rest of us. She wanted to remember Emma as a vibrant, perky young woman, and had no interest in sitting next to her comatose daughter, watching her die along with everyone else. A few people grumbled about her indifference, but I thought her logic was normal.

Thomas stayed by Emma's side, as well as her brothers, Bryan and Nate. Occasionally Anthony or Joey would come in to whisper in their mother's ear. Then, they'd go back with their grandmother to the privacy of the waiting room down the hall.

Ken came to the hospital that afternoon and sat next to me, holding my hand. In all of his years working in the mental health field as a crisis counselor, he'd never seen a death-watch like that one. No one paid any attention to him, of course. He was, after all, a *worldly* man. Not a *man of God*, as an elder later categorized him. Oh, but he *was* a man of God, much more so than one hypocritical elder who finally removed his mask of Christian love and kindness, three weeks later.

His name was Aiden Munroe—tall, relatively handsome, with a radio-announcer voice. When Aiden Munroe spoke, everyone listened. I'd known him ever since moving to Louisville some twenty-seven years before. I thought I could trust him with my concerns, so I told him I'd been spiritually weak and had some doubts I'd like to discuss. I planned to come back to the Woodlawn Hall after Emma's death and I asked him if he could help me. He thought it was a good idea, even though I lived in Indiana and Woodlawn was in Louisville, but for a period of time maybe I could give it a try. During the next three weeks I prayed constantly, asking Jehovah to please help me understand why I was no longer wholehearted about The Truth.

I told Emma I loved her and said goodbye, but she was non-responsive. I was sure she would pass away during the night. I would have loved the chance to give her a proper good-bye—not over the telephone. I would've gone to see her and sat beside her bed. According to Thomas, she wanted to save me the anguish because she knew I was still grieving for my mother. Losing them both was the most painful thing I'd ever known. But it didn't end there.

CHAPTER FORTY-FOUR
ANYWHERE BUT HERE

"Leadership is a privilege to better the lives of others. It is not an opportunity to satisfy personal greed." ~ *Mwai Kibaki*

I explained to Enos my plan to drive across the river for the meetings. He understood I needed a spiritual boost—if I thought Woodlawn would meet my needs, go for it. We'd been riding to the meetings together, but he had a dependable car, so I wasn't deserting him. He drove several days a week out in the ministry work, as he had continued to pioneer after my mother's death the year before.

Toward the end of August, I psyched myself up for my new spiritual infusion and headed over to the Woodlawn Hall one Sunday morning. A long time friend of mine, Laura, accompanied me. Laura had been disfellowshipped and reinstated a year or two before at our Indiana congregation. She had similar frustrations with the aftermath of her experience, somewhat like mine. She thought going to Woodlawn might be a nice change for herself, as well.

I enjoyed that meeting more than any I could remember during the past two years. Everywhere I looked, my old friends seemed genuinely glad I was back at Woodlawn. No one seemed to care I'd been twice divorced and was married to a non-Witness. They all treated me with compassion and kindness, just like the old Woodlawn I'd spent so much time with. I noticed the wallpaper inserts on the front stage that Emma and I had hung years before. I participated during that Watchtower Study with ease—finally at home.

After the meeting, I chatted with Lydia, Anthony and Joey, and finally walked over into the middle of an aisle where Thomas stood. We had a short conversation and he was happy to learn I'd be attending meetings there. I went home that day, optimistic for my future. I was "keeping my eyes on the prize" again, feeling confident that Aiden Munroe and the other elders would assist me toward that endeavor.

~*~

When you answer the phone, it's rarely a good thing when someone asks if you're sitting down. On Wednesday evening, I received a phone call from Brother Graham in Indiana. He said Aiden Munroe had called and asked him to inform me that the "elder body" at Woodlawn had decided they didn't want me to attend there. Munroe referred to a "suspiciously private" conversation I'd had with Thomas at Sunday's meeting, and their alleged decision hinged on a certain phone call I'd had with Emma where I told her I planned to marry Thomas after she died! "Go back to your Indiana congregation to repair your spirituality, or any other Kingdom Hall. Anywhere but here."

As soon as we disconnected, I immediately picked up the phone and called Aiden Munroe to get to the root of this farce. His icy voice was razor-sharp, not loving in any way. I would not allow myself to be treated this way and spoke to Munroe with a calm voice. I didn't want a confrontation, but a conversation about this issue was in order.

Apparently Hannah, a "friend" of Emma's, had felt it her duty to inform Thomas that Emma had been upset with me because I had a casual attitude about remarriage and had joked about marrying Thomas myself. I couldn't remember telling Emma anything like that, and I knew I certainly had no intention of such a thing. Slowly, however, the memory of that phone conversation came back to me. All this drama caused from one silly statement I'd made *six months* before. Unbelievable, and yet it was happening. Why hadn't Hannah told me Emma was upset? I could've smoothed things over. I was never given the chance because I had no idea there was a problem. To consider that Emma was seriously bothered by my words wrenched my gut. I sobbed and bawled throughout the night and all the next day. This was exactly what a broken heart felt like.

Ken, furious that a so-called Christian organization would handle a personal matter in this fashion, encouraged me to do whatever necessary to straighten it out. I made dozens of phone calls: Hannah, Emma's brothers and parents, and finally to Thomas.

Thomas's response was that Hannah claimed Emma had been upset, and he was troubled that Emma kept something from him while she was ill. He'd asked Aiden Munroe to look into it since he didn't understand what was going on. Thomas made it clear that he did not want me to leave Woodlawn —he'd never suggested that, nor was he aware I'd been ordered to stay away.

Of *course* Emma hadn't told Thomas about our conversation; she wouldn't want him to know she'd shared the fact about his roughness with the boys and she worried about their safety. Now was not the time to bring it up, either. The man had just lost his wife—this was another heartache I would protect him from.

Hannah claimed she had to shelter Thomas for Emma's sake. *She was thinking of what Emma would want?* "Well great," I said. "I'm sure Emma would be grateful for your help, especially since her husband is now terribly confused and distressed. Look at what you've done!" I reminded her of her Christian obligation to make sure a misunderstanding is managed appropriately, according to the scriptures. Emma and I were *both* her Christian sisters—she owed it to each of us, not only Emma. Her response? She didn't think it had been six months since Emma had told her about our conversation. What did *that* have to do with it? I didn't think the Bible set a timetable on these matters. The sooner, the better, when handling misunderstandings.

I talked to Aiden Munroe again, pleading to be allowed to supply the details and the foundation of that phone call. He adamantly refused to listen, insisted the phone call was NOT six months ago, (like *he* would know) and would not hear anything I had to say because, "The only person who could tell us what really was said is dead." (Can you believe *that*?) "We're all mourning the loss of a dear sister here and your presence won't help." They couldn't keep me away, of course, but it would be better for all concerned if I didn't step foot in the door, he'd said. It sounded like a threat to me.

The halo one wears for refusing a blood transfusion in a life-threatening situation apparently has a time limit. I'd lost my hero status at Woodlawn. I'd been arrested, found guilty and sentenced, unaware my trial was in progress! Another judgment based merely on the perception of gossipmongers who had no idea what they were talking about.

I called Emma's brothers, Bryan and Nate. They assured me Emma was not unhappy with me. Two days before she lost consciousness, Emma told Nate she trusted me to look after her boys.

Finally, I spoke to Lydia and Emma's father. I hated to bother them with this, but they wanted to know what was going on. Lydia gently reminded me that Emma loved me dearly and had *never* indicated she was troubled about anything I'd ever said to her. She explained that as sick as Emma was, sometimes toward the end she would say things they knew she didn't really mean.

Emma's father spoke clearly. "Listen to me, JoEmma. There's been no elder meeting or a group decision about you. I'm an elder here at Woodlawn, and if there had been a meeting, I would've known about it." Yes, they were aware of Thomas's temper, and yes they planned to look after the boys, so not to worry about that. "Get yourself back to Woodlawn, JoEmma. You hear me?"

Hmmm. There had been no elder meeting after all. Why had I been lied to? Aiden Munroe had made the decision entirely on his own. He was the Presiding Overseer and took it upon himself to make a serious judgment, something that supposedly was not allowed in an Organization which touted that group decisions would be made lovingly, with evidence presented by all concerned. Thomas had asked Munroe to handle it, so he did just that. Cast me out, he did!

What were Hannah's motives for waiting until after Emma died, after she'd heard that I was going to Woodlawn, to tell Thomas three weeks after his wife's death of a conversation that had taken place months before? Was she trying to warn him to be careful of me, a married woman old enough to be his mother? What a joke. Perhaps she wanted him for herself, although she was married at the time, as well. If she'd been as truly concerned as she claimed to be, the appropriate channel would have been to discuss her concerns with an elder at Woodlawn, not the widower. How impulsive, rude and unthinking to bother a freshly widowed man with that five-pound bag of shit in a three-pound bag, as Enos had always described a "mess" with an adorable impish grin on his face.

CHAPTER FORTY-FIVE
YOU IGNORED MY REQUEST, AGAIN?

What about the previous three weeks of prayer to Jehovah, beseeching Him to help me understand why I was no longer happy in The Truth? He'd ignored me, just like on the day I was baptized when He wouldn't check "yes" or "no" on my handwritten prayer. I had to make my own decision, when most of my life the Organization made them for me.

Laura, who had been there with me at Woodlawn that day, suggested Jehovah had answered my prayer, "Obviously you're not going to get the help here that you've asked for. I think He's telling you get the hell out and find another way."

I recalled the Kingdom Melody, Take Sides with Jehovah: "*Take sides with Jehovah, make Him your delight. He'll never forsake you . . . .*" It sure felt like I'd been forsaken by my friend Jehovah. So, was His answer this: "*Walk out the opened door, remove your blinders, and see the world and your life for what it actually is, and not for what a group of mortal men want it to be.*"

I couldn't believe God would direct me in that manner, however I soon realized that if my desire was strong enough, it wouldn't matter what my beliefs were. The desire would be the dominant vibration and would override any other vibration that I had, including a lifetime of beliefs. Laura was right, and partly because of what happened to me, she decided to leave The Truth. She had wavered with her annoyance of the Organization's tactics long enough; this was the catalyst she needed.

In the following weeks, my emotions traveled back and forth. Should I leave or should I stay? Enos was the biggest cheerleader for a "staying" verdict. "What Brother Munroe did was wrong," he said. "Don't let *anyone* stumble you from serving Jehovah!" Enos begged me to attend meetings at the Kingdom Hall with him and let the brothers and sisters in my own congregation help me attain a higher level of spiritual health. "Stick with the Lowland Congregation," Enos said, "Forget Woodlawn!"

Lydia and Anthony met me after school one afternoon in September to give me Emma's charm bracelet. I would attach my charms next to hers and create a JoEmma bracelet. They urged me to return to Woodlawn and ignore what Brother Munroe or anyone else thought. "Whatever you do, please don't leave the truth," Anthony pleaded. My dear Anthony, a fourteen year old young man, duplicated his mother's concern and compassion within his heart. I knew what Emma would want.

Brother Graham, who'd called to tell me I'd better be sitting down, offered peculiar suggestions. "I've been thinking about your dilemma," he said. "I sincerely realize how painful this is for you, so you can do one of three things, in my opinion, if Woodlawn is your final choice. You can attend meetings there and sit with Emma's family but not next to Thomas; or you can go and sit anywhere you please, but only talk to Thomas when he's with a crowd of people or his family; or you can take Ken with you and let the whole congregation see you're happily married with no hidden agenda."

Something about those ideas didn't set right with me. Recall, I was married to a *worldly* man who had been right by my side during Emma's death-watch. The entire congregation was stuffed into her hospital room at one time or another that afternoon. Had no one noticed I was a married woman then? And why should I expect my *not-a-man-of-god* husband to attend a Kingdom Hall when he had his own worldly church to go to? I talked these ideas over with Ken.

"I'll go with you if you want," Ken said, "but it seems like game-playing to me."

Ah-ha! Game playing! Sit where I'm told, talk to specific people, and keep my man on a short leash by my side. Follow the rules of the game. Always look straight ahead, never to the left or right, keep my eyes on the prize. But which prize? Should I pick door number one, door number two, or door number three?

Decisions, decisions. I finally picked door number four—stay away from *all* Kingdom Halls! If Jehovah's Witnesses were, in fact, God's one and only Organization, The Truth, they would not allow one of their sheep to be inhumanely devoured by a wolf-like elder. Brother Graham's game-playing ideas really bothered me, too, even though I knew he was merely trying to help. But the manipulative nature of his suggestions added the cherry to the whipped cream. Woodlawn wasn't the only congregation with players for leaders.

I have not stepped through the door of a Kingdom Hall since that decisive August day in 1997.

CHAPTER FORTY-SIX
REGRETS

"Regrets, I've had a few. But then again, too few to mention." ~ Frank Sinatra's song "I Did It My Way"

I regret my know-it-all attitude as an eighteen-year-old new wife back in 1966, and I'm sorry for some of the things I said and did to Jim through the years. I wish I'd made the time to talk to Emma about that life-changing telephone conversation. And I am disappointed in myself for impulsively calling Jim on his wedding day, even though my intentions were innocent. So, sure I have regrets, but my decision to leave The Truth when the end was still nowhere in sight was not one of them, although that failed prophecy was not why I walked away. If I *believed* it, nothing could have slowed me down.

I had difficulty helping Enos understand this. When one is brain-trained, their blinders prevent focusing on one side or the other—they see only what's immediately in front of them. I don't think he ever really understood, and it tore me in half to disappoint him, but I had to be true to myself.

Several elders knew of my predicament, yet Aiden Munroe was not disciplined for his deceit. He didn't call to apologize or explain further, even though he was advised that his actions *stumbled* me. He apparently wasn't worried about the scripture at Matthew 18:6: "But whoever stumbles one of these little ones who put faith in me, it is more beneficial for him to have hung around his neck a millstone such as is turned by an ass and to be sunk in the wide, open sea." Munroe is currently the *Congregation Coordinator* at the Woodlawn Congregation of Jehovah's Witnesses. That position was previously termed *Presiding Overseer*, but the Society changes the names and titles of things ever-so-often to make it look fresh and new. It's all semantics.

The Organization has a favorite word—*debauchery*—repeatedly warning that those who leave The Truth invariably head back into the world toward a miserable lifestyle of debauchery. Maybe that happens to some, but my behavior didn't disintegrate, nor was I miserable; I was positive about my choice. I'd already survived a previous mid-life crisis and found I liked myself better when practicing good morals.

Those who knew what had happened, or *thought* they did, insisted I'd been spiritually stumbled. I'll admit, the events leading up to my exit tripped me, but if I hadn't already had my foot on the threshold, the door wouldn't have swung open so fast and slammed shut as hard behind me.

I faced a different way of life without religion, and I was frustrated and didn't know where to turn. Frustration and confusion because I had left behind a belief system which I had trusted, one in which I'd felt safe, and moved into an arena where I had to make my own rules. Had all of my questions been answered? I used to believe it, until I slipped out of the parentheses and discovered not a single one of the answers was suitable for me any longer. I no longer knew it all. In fact, I knew nothing true for sure. I had been on the inside looking out; now I was on the outside looking *around*, but never back in. It had been ingrained in me that my religion was the one and only, so where did I stand with God now that I was no longer a part of it? Was there actually a god who cared?

Life was often blinding without the blinders on!

CHAPTER FORTY-SEVEN
DEATH—WHO KNOWS?

"I have found that making peace with where I am is easier when I've made peace with where everyone else is, even those who choose not to associate with me any longer." ~ Chapter Fifty-Two

When someone we love dies, we have to redefine ourselves all over again without them in our life . . . only in our memory. Our behavior mirrors what we are inside. Therefore, when someone dies and we're busy redefining ourselves, we might not know who or what we are and our behavior reflects that confusion. Although I don't usually hang out with funeral directors, I have had a conversation with one or two, and the general consensus is that people act in unpredictable ways when they're faced with the death of a loved one. They hurry and scurry, trying to be in control of themselves and *others*, when they are actually so out of control it hurts. And when it hurts, the feeling is similar to some kind of horrible fear. The fear of your own death, perhaps? With that said, who can safely blame anyone for anything they did wrong?

I can't.

I've learned not to blame others for my difficulties. It keeps the cycle of the past right up in my face so the present can't be enjoyed to the fullest as it is now—today. Moreover, I don't consider my time spent as a Jehovah's Witness to be a mistake or a waste of time. What would be the point to that? To the contrary, allowing the past to take up space in one's mind is a genuine time-waster. Bad memories are valuable only when used as life experiences, to make adjustments in our current lifestyles. I eventually learned to take what I gained while in The Truth and use it to my best advantage. I acknowledge the parts of my experience that helped shape my personality and offered me a cocoon of safety while growing up.

But considering how it all crumbled at the end, I had plenty of anger to sort out until I learned to release blame. Ken shared an enlightening thought: no matter what a person does, even if it is for the good of someone else, their real motive is to make themselves feel better, or at least it always turns out that way even if they aren't aware of it. I agreed; we feel good when we do good for others, so we both benefit, and I saw no harm in that.

My therapist suggested that Aiden Munroe's injudicious actions reminded her of one who'd witnessed incest. Had he viewed me as a mother figure in Emma's life, horrified that I would suggest marrying Thomas? I scoffed at the idea at first, until I remembered something I'd heard in confidence a few years before about Munroe. It began to make sense to me and I *almost* felt compassion for that man but could not excuse him for equating his personal problems with the individuals in his congregation, if, in fact, that's what he had done. He was commissioned to watch out for the best interests of God's sheep, not to look through the filters of the skeletons in his own family closet.

CHAPTER FORTY-EIGHT
HERE WE GO (AGAIN)

"I don't have to think—I'm a Catholic!" ~Kathleen Turner
from the movie, The Perfect Family

Ken gave me a C. S. Lewis book, *Mere Christianity*. He thought it would clarify things for me and he suggested we attend his Christian church together. I went with him a few times, but I'd become unsure of the existence of God. I was also dealing with the effects of long-time training and brainwashing that I'd suffered regarding Babylon the Great, the World Empire of False Religion, made up primarily of Christendom—religions claiming to be Christian. I kept thinking, *There is nowhere else to go to worship God. Nowhere.* Then, I questioned that word *worship*. Why would a god actually require it? Appreciation, for sure. But worship? I knew more about what I didn't believe than what I did. One thing I knew for a certainty: I did *not* want to be a hypocrite. I didn't like the effect it had on the ones I'd been spending most of my time with all of my life.

During the following months, I became aware of my previously veiled political and religious opinions, ones I'd never voiced. I'd kept them within those parentheses, even away from my own consciousness. But now, everything tumbled from the secret closet. Unfortunately for our marriage, my convictions and principles were in direct conflict with Ken's. We disagreed on the basic fundamentals of religion, politics, money and business. Our relationship sadly disintegrated, as we had little in common and could barely remember what had attracted us in the beginning. We agreed we'd function better as good friends than as husband and wife.

Ken has remained a valued friend of my family, and since he doesn't have children or grandchildren of his own, Greta and Jackson manage to keep him busy in the "Grandpa Ken" department, accompanying him to museums, hot-air balloon races and movies. He attends Greta's soccer and Jackson's basketball games. They help him select his live Christmas tree and decorate it every year. It's gratifying to see them spending time together.

~*~

146

Not all divorces bring pain, but having gone through my third, I labeled myself as a three-time loser, and the familiar guilt of failure weighed heavily on me. Okay, maybe they weren't *failed* marriages, because I had learned valuable lessons from each, but they had ended and I knew I played a large part in the demise of all three. I was a hopeless romantic, helplessly in need of a good quality man, but I doubted there were any available to take a chance on me. I knew what caused my divorces—marriage. I resolved never to marry again. Maybe a torrid love affair someday, but never another wedding.

~*~

We sold the house and I moved back across the river to Louisville. I realized I'd made a bad decision almost immediately, because it felt like I'd abandoned Enos, even though I drove over two or three times each week. His nephew Jim, my ex, looked in on Enos regularly and I knew he was in good hands all the way around, but he confided that he missed having me right next door. I brought home-cooked meals and groceries and paid his bills as we visited at his kitchen table. Many of our short discussions started out with his asking a question: when was I going to come back to meetings? He was obviously frustrated with my decision and persuaded himself that it was temporary. One day he said, "What am I going to tell your mother when she's resurrected and you're not there? What about the promises you made when she was dying?"

I sat quietly for a moment, determined to retain my composure. Finally, I managed to say, "What makes you think I won't be there? Who are *you* to judge me?"

"Well . . . you know what I mean," he mumbled.

That's why our discussions were short. We had nothing much to talk about once his pantry was organized, bills were paid, and other formalities were out of the way, such as chats about the weather and family. Enos never failed to say he loved me and how much he appreciated everything I did for him. I'd looked after him since Mom died because I'd promised her I would. I grew closer to him as an individual, not just as my mother's husband. I loved him very much, and he never failed to wave a cheerful goodbye, standing at his front door as I backed out of his driveway. I was often overcome with tears because I'd never meant to disappoint him.

Every time I pulled into Enos' drive, I looked over at my old house and felt a pang of grief for having abandoned a home I'd put so much love and thought into. I'd made one of those spur-of-the-moment decisions one is never supposed to make within the first year after a family tragedy such as death or divorce. Eventually, I discovered Julia Cameron's favorite quote, "Leap and the net will appear." In my case, the net did appear. My house went back on the market and I bought it! How often does something like that happen? The family to whom I'd sold the house had outgrown it after six years. It was as though they'd been house-sitting, giving me time to get my act together.

~*~

I'd been living in a stately, brick three-story apartment building, The Monserrat, at 851 South Fourth Street in downtown Louisville, a structure with a remarkable history. Built in 1857, it was originally used as The Fifth Ward School. Its cavernous basement had been an Underground Railway stop to hide runaway slaves. During the Civil War, it served as a Union hospital. After the war, the school was reopened and the building was renamed "The Monserrat School" for its dearly-loved principal. After her death in 1900, the facility continued educating young ones until 1940. During WWII, the building functioned as a dorm for soldiers on leave from Ft. Knox. Later, the Natural History Museum of the Louisville Free Public Library moved in, housing an Egyptian mummy. After the museum moved to a new location, it was finally transformed into upscale apartments. Each unit was a unique, architectural delight with fourteen-foot arched windows, angled walls and magnificent woodwork.

I was told that some of my neighbors weren't real, as the old building was known for housing ghosts: a mummy, a young slave and soldiers. I lived on the top floor with tall vaulted ceilings and a bedroom loft accessed by a spiral staircase, but ineffective air-conditioning brought with it a sense of suffocation. The ceiling fan, though helpful, invariably shut itself off around midnight. My live neighbors reported similar occurrences, but the maintenance man could never find a solution. I figured one or more of the ghosts had developed a ritual of turning the fans off, just for kicks.

I'd divided my employment between medical transcription and bookkeeping, when I decided to learn more in-depth accounting techniques. I found a part-time job as an accountant's assistant in downtown Louisville near my haunted apartment, and I registered for classes at a local technical school.

~*~

148

I was at my new job for less than a month, when he walked into my office. I stood at a filing cabinet and glanced up to see who had entered the room: an HVAC service technician was there to repair a non-functioning air-conditioning unit on the fifth floor. He smiled, said hello, and asked if the accountant was in. I directed him to the adjacent office and watched as he walked into it. He sported a thick, dark beard, wore baggy blue jeans and a royal blue work-shirt with "Craig" on his embroidered nametag. He showed no trace of a wedding ring. As I went on with my work, I overheard everything he and Carol, my supervisor, talked about. There was something about his voice; it sang to me. Carol introduced us for the sake of professional etiquette and Craig went on his way to the fifth floor. "That Craig is such a *nice* guy," Carol said. "He's fixed our furnace for years at my house."

"Is he married?"

"Umm . . . no. He's divorced."

"Ah," I said. I asked her if he had a girlfriend and she said, "How would *I* know?"

"You could ask him—just take the elevator up with some other excuse and work it into the conversation."

"What grade of elementary school are we in, here?" Carol snickered. "No. Absolutely not! I introduced you; now it's up to you."

Craig returned to our office and I did everything short of a belly dance to attract his attention. I babbled on about the faulty air-conditioning in my apartment, and I asked Craig for advice. I didn't include the part about the ghosts. Rather than offering to come and take a look, help a single girl fix her thermostat, he merely gave me detailed instructions to fix it myself. Was this man daft? If not, I figured he must have a girlfriend.

Drat! Now what? I stomped around, trying to think of some way to talk to Craig again. My physician had recently prescribed hormone replacement for the side effects of menopause, and Carol and another co-worker threatened to hold an intervention to wean me off the drugs! They both laughed and joked about my desire to meet Craig, but I wasn't joking at all. I knew I'd find a way, sooner or later.

On my way out of the office, I rounded the corner at the elevator station, and who did I see but Glen, the Maintenance Supervisor. I'd seen him in the parking lot during lunchtime with Craig.

"Well, hey, Glen!" I said. "Do you know that HVAC guy who was here earlier?"

"Oh, yeah, I've known Craig a long time."

"Well . . . I wonder if he has a girlfriend."

"Hah! Funny you should ask," Glen said. "We were just talking about that earlier. Yep, he sure does, but he's trying to get rid of her!"

"Perhaps I can help," I said.

His face took on an expression of enlightenment and it appeared as though he might jump for joy. He offered to give Craig my phone number.

"Yes, do that, and tell him I'd like to go out on a date and I don't want to wait around forever!"

When I saw his name on Caller ID that evening, I couldn't believe Craig was so punctual. I gave him extra points for that. "Hello, this is your friendly service man," Craig said. We talked for an hour, and the following evenings we talked for at least two hours. Two weeks later, we had our first date at a restaurant down the street from The Monserrat. When he noticed my white 1993 Cutlass convertible, he told me he'd give me extra points for it. There we were, both racking up points!

Another month went by, and when he didn't call, I reckoned he must have preferred to stay with his girlfriend, but as it turned out, July and August were insane months for commercial air-conditioner repairmen. He'd untangled himself from his prior relationship and we became a couple. What surprised me was when I asked him if he'd shave his beard, the next time I saw him it was gone! Even more surprising was when I realized I liked him better with it, he grew it back. More points for him!

One of the first subjects we undertook in many of our intellectual conversations was my prior religion, how I "fell out of it" the year before and was still stumbling along, seeking closure. Craig had discovered his "meaning of life and religion" at the young age of eighteen, while in the army in Germany during the Vietnam conflict. He gave me the names of books that he'd found helpful, and I was glad to take a look at those. Craig thought reincarnation was a strong possibility, he believed in energy of the human spirit, and he was probably one of the most honest and straightforward men I'd ever had the privilege to spend time with. The only thing we disagreed on was the existence of God. I desperately *wanted* to believe in God.

CHAPTER FORTY-NINE
DEATH IS A BITCH OVER THE PHONE

A few weeks after I met Craig, I was dining with my cousin and a group of his church friends (not JWs) at a Chinese bistro. I held the mobile phone tightly to my right ear and stuck a finger in the other—a vain attempt to drown out background noise.

"Dad is dead," Jesse said.

"WHAT?"

Sixteen chopsticks suspended in mid-air; eight total strangers at my table stared at me. I had yelled, not as though I hadn't heard my son correctly —oh, I'd heard him all right—but his message was unfathomable!

Jesse spat out the same words, "I *said* Dad's dead. They think it was a heart attack. Carolyn found him lying beside his old tractor a couple hours ago."

I stared at my phone. Caller ID read HOME, and since I'd left Jordan there alone, to hear Jesse's voice confused me. What was he doing at my house? All three of my sons sounded alike, so was it Jordan or Jesse? Was this someone's idea of a joke?

"Who *is* this?" I demanded.

"It's Jesse. Dad died," he said flatly. "Mom . . . you need to come home."

Jesse had a history of prank telephone calls, but I knew this was not one of them. My brain raced to hell and back, my neck was on fire, my arms lost strength and I couldn't get enough air.

"Does Jordan know?" I squeaked.

"Yes. I'm with him. Mom do you understand me? Really, you need to come home right away."

I ached to burst into tears that wouldn't materialize. I stood up and told my cousin the tragic news—asked him to please take me home to my sons *immediately*. He rose to his feet but his wife pulled him back down, insisting we all have a prayer. Everyone held hands, and the next thing I knew, a woman I'd met not thirty minutes before grabbed my arm and I found myself back in my chair. She prayed out loud, but her entreaty did nothing for me other than cause angst and annoyance. Maybe it helped the rest of them.

I'd heard thousands of prayers in my lifetime, but never had endured a longer one. She went on, continually repeating herself, while I thought of my little boys, who really weren't little anymore at all, without me there, and this horrible news about their father. I had always been there for them before. A gasket in my cranium was ready to pop, trapped as I was, and while I was loathe to interrupt her circular conversation with the Divine, I seriously considered the prospect. At last, she said Amen. Everyone else repeated her Amen, and I said (to myself) Praise the Lord! With all due respect, I'm sure she had nothing but the best of intentions. *God love her* (as my Grandma always used to say), she'd been put on the spot herself. I mean, how often does something like that happen?

Jim wasn't a farmer, per se, but he and Carolyn owned some acreage upon which they planned to build a fine white farmhouse during retirement. They had a scale model architectural mock-up of it displayed in the entry foyer of their business. I guess if he had to die at the young age of fifty, a fitting place would be right next to his dearly-loved Massey Ferguson. I tried to wrap my head around it. Okay, sure. He'd been mowing the fields in the hot, August sun. He'd stepped off the tractor, was stricken with a heart attack, and unable to reach his cell phone, died instantly. I hoped he hadn't suffered; you never stop loving the father of your children.

I didn't know why Jesse had come to my house that night, but he'd taken the message over the phone from Carolyn's son, and he'd made several phone calls of his own to verify the information before telling Jordan. I was relieved Jordan hadn't taken the phone call; what a sad scenario that would have been for a fifteen-year-old boy at home alone.

I inserted the key to my front door, dreading to face them. I knew what they were feeling, as the similarities were so painfully obvious; my dad died suddenly of a heart attack at the same young age. I put my arms around Jesse, patted him on the back like people do in these situations, as though that says it all. I went for Jordan's bedroom. He was playing a video game. He glanced up, saw me standing in his doorway, but continued his game.

"I'm so sorry," I said.

"About what?" He kept playing, didn't miss a move.

"About . . . Dad."

He shrugged his shoulders, one a little higher than the other. He mumbled something like, "Whatever," but I wasn't sure what he meant.

Denial, I thought. Although I knew I should cross the room and hug my son, his body language indicated he did not need or want one. If he'd been alone when the phone call came, would he have called me, or casually gone on playing his video games?

There would've been more hugging if their dad and I had never been divorced; it would have been a *family* mourning time. And I wondered, why couldn't I cry? Why . . . no one was crying for that matter, as though we were numb. It didn't occur to me at first that I was now a single mother—the only parent my three sons had. I'd always thought of Jim as a steel anchor for the boys; I had no idea what I was in for. I knew from now on I would also be the only one responsible for making sure Enos was taken care of as he aged further.

With Jesse and Jordan accounted for, I tracked Jason down. He'd gone to a party in the adjacent county and I left a message for him to call his mother. When he called, I told him about his father and wished I could have been there to tell him in person. I knew firsthand hearing bad news over the phone just plain sucks.

When all three boys were together, they drove to their dad's home for the rest of the night. By then, Jim's parents and siblings had arrived from Indianapolis, and my boys belonged with them, to be comforted by their father's family—aunts, uncles, grandparents and cousins. Enos was there, too, of course.

I didn't belong with them; I was the one who had thrown the marriage away. It was past midnight, and I was left alone to sit and think in my quiet, dark home. My first thoughts were of myself, not an unusual thing, since I was the only one there. I wondered how this would affect me monetarily, for Jim had paid maintenance and child support and was scheduled to do so for several more years. Single and on my own—working part-time and attending college—without Jim's financial input everything would change. I also wondered how the boys would deal with the death of their father. I told myself to be strong and help them work through it.

I couldn't fathom the concept that the man who had helped me bring these three wonderful young men into the world was gone. *It just isn't fair*, I thought. *I'm still here and he isn't. He won't be here to see Greta experience her first birthday cake next month.*

At one o'clock in the morning my phone rang. It was Jason, the bearer of more bad news. The family had waited until all three of them were there to tell them the truth, the whole story. Maybe it was a heart attack, or heat stroke, but since the old tractor had been produced in the days before automatic safety shut-offs to stop it in the event the driver fell off, it had continued on its path with Jim's powerful, new bush hog following behind. Jim's body had been discovered by Carolyn, not *beside* his tractor, but mangled underneath the sharp, round mower blades.

Carolyn was under sedation; my heart was heavy with sadness for her. She'd assured Jason their father died instantly from a heart attack, but for a reason I never understood, she did not allow the Medical Examiner to order an autopsy. I knew this heart attack theory could never be proven. Jim's wife had chosen in a split second to believe it and to soothe the boys with the assumption. I guess they bought it. I told myself it had to be true.

This new bit of information added an entirely new dimension to the situation. *Now I could cry*. In the dark, still alone, I longed for my children, even though they weren't babies anymore, but as their mother it was essential for me to hold them whether they needed it or not. I think I wanted some hugs, myself. But who would have ever believed such a thing? We were divorced; no one would understand my agony. Had Jim felt the horror, the pain of dying?

I wept freely through the night as I remembered our wedding day, thirty-two years ago, when I walked out of the dressing room toward Jim who took his bride's hand and said, "Here we go."

CHAPTER FIFTY
DIVORCE WITHOUT A TISSUE

Music from the past drifted through the darkened room. Billy Joel's *Honesty*, boomed from a tape deck Jim had secretly installed in a brand new 1979 Olds Cutlass as a surprise for me. Ten years later, Phil Collins' *Throwing It All Away,* had played on the radio as I drove the long fifteen miles to the courthouse on the day of our divorce. Surely the song was a sign. Was I throwing it all away? I'd cried and dug into my purse for a tissue, but I hadn't thought to bring one. Despondent and overwhelmed with gloom, I wondered if I was doing the right thing. I couldn't remember one good reason I'd wanted a divorce, and when I showed up at the courthouse, there was no one for support other than my lawyer, and even he hadn't brought a tissue. One would think an attorney would carry a cotton handkerchief!

Like a slideshow, the images of our divorce filtered through my consciousness in the middle of that horrible night. I'd read a newspaper article during the period when our lawyers scampered gaily about, back and forth, billing by the minute, documents to be signed, or not, argued and re-written. The article warned divorce participants as to how long it takes to recover from the trauma. It was well-written and made sense, but I'd scoffed at the idea, because I'd wanted the divorce so badly I couldn't imagine getting *over* it—I wanted to get *on* with it. Nine years had passed, and while I'd gone about my merry way, just as Jim had seemed to do, I had never done my *grief work* regarding our split. I had never felt the need, whereas now my grief sat heavily next to me on my bed in the blackness and could no longer be ignored.

I'd watched Jim walk in, head held high, down the hallway toward the courtroom, his posse by his side, a complete support team of six: an elder from my prior congregation; Jerry and Barbara; Jim's business partner Leroy Kellems; Jim's secretary—soon-to-be next wife; and JoAnn—my favorite sister-in-law. (She was my favorite for many reasons, particularly because she had taken me aside, years ago, and graphically explained to me how a woman reaches orgasm.)

How humiliating for me; they were all there on *his* side. I didn't think to bring my own support team and had been unable to stop crying. Finally a natty old man sympathetically handed me a tissue while we were waiting in the hallway. I saw him later in the courtroom, and I couldn't believe they put my divorce on trial in front of all those creepy thieves and drug dealers. I continued to sob through the whole procedure, and since my lawyer had secured more tissues, we made it through. The judge wore an expression of real concern when he asked me if I was sure this was what I wanted. Jim had already warned me that if I changed my mind, he would continue the proceedings, so what was the point? I couldn't back down with everyone's eyes upon me. There were those criminals waiting for their trials, for heaven's sakes. Admitting my own defeat, I simply wanted other people in the courtroom to move on with their day.

Afterward, I went out with friends for drinks, supposedly to celebrate my divorce, while Jim packed his personal belongings and moved temporarily out of our home, waiting for my new place to become available. My mom was at home with our boys, and Jim had sat down and talked to her, said during the court proceedings he watched me and thought, "She is the most beautiful woman I've ever known."

I grunted. "I noticed him staring but clearly did not pick up on *that* vibe. He told me when I filed for divorce no one would ever love me the way he did, but Mom, I haven't felt beautiful or loved for a long time."

"I'll always love you," Mom said.

"I know, Mom. But I needed to feel loved by my life partner, yet Jim discounted nearly every intelligent thing I ever said, as though he always knew better, or more, than I did."

Mom nodded. "I noticed. It always infuriated me when he didn't show you the respect you deserved."

I shrugged. "That's the way he was. Other people saw it, too. I guess it's what Enos meant when he said he never knew why I'd married Jim."

Our marriage counselor likened Jim to the ever-negative Eeyore, whereas I was a bouncy Tigger. I'd described my dissatisfaction as a *hole in my heart* to our therapist, who implied the void had nothing to do with my marriage, but with my childhood. I strongly disagreed with his psychobabble.

~*~

I remained in the shadows of that night of Jim's death. He was gone and I tried to remember, *why did I leave him? Why hadn't I calmly sat down nine years ago and dissected the meaning of those words with him, lyrics from the song he likened our marriage to, "Send In The Clowns," rather than merely wonder which parts he thought each of us played. Now I would never know.* Jim had been angry when I wanted a divorce and wouldn't communicate with me afterward about anything except our children. Whether or not I did the right thing didn't matter because he remarried so quickly there was no time for second thoughts. He'd asked for the house with the divorce. What if I hadn't agreed? Would he have bought a newer tractor, one with a safety shut-off? Surely I must be to blame, somehow. If we hadn't divorced would he still be alive?

Very early the following morning, Jesse, Jason and I went to Jim's farm. "Carolyn might not want to see you on her property under the circumstances," Jason warned, "but I want you to be with us."

"I'll ride in the back seat and stay in the car if it seems appropriate—if anyone else is there," I said. The very last thing I wanted was to upset Jim's widow. Jason pulled onto the grass-covered driveway; no other vehicles were in sight. He slowly made his way until we saw the Massey-Ferguson in the field off to our right. It had apparently kept chugging along until it collided head-on with a large, round bale of hay. I morbidly wondered how far it would've dragged Jim's body if there'd been no obstruction present.

We shuffled across the newly-mowed, dew-covered lawn. The bush-hog was detached, resting several feet away from the tractor. It showed no signs of suffering or pain, for which we were relieved; the authorities had apparently hosed it down. We stood close to the spot where Jim had undoubtedly taken his last breath, wishing we could turn back time sixteen hours and change the unspeakable moment.

It was then I noticed a bright red substance on the ground. I pressed with the toe of my sneaker and found an underlying reddish wetness on the soggy ground. Taking a step back, I stooped down and touched a single blade of grass. Standing there, staring at the red dot on my fingertip, I had a momentary flashback of the horror of the scene, fully grasping the violence of his death. *This is all there is left of him?* I nearly doubled over, unable to stop guttural moans which seemed to be coming from my throat, but I refused to stop looking at Jim's blood.

"Mom!" Jason screamed. "What are you doing? Don't you know what that is?"

What is he saying? Of course I know what this is. It's the soul of the boy who carried microphones at the Kingdom Hall at the young age of fifteen; who combed his hair funny; who caught my eye; who fathered my children; who taught me to drive a stick-shift; who loved his mother's cooking; who thought I was the most beautiful woman he'd ever seen.

Jim's blood had captured my heart. How could he be gone and yet a vital part of him remain with me? I knew exactly what the red substance was —it was the soul of my soul-mate. For twenty-three years we created a mixed box of unresolved communication issues. Then, he died, leaving me to clean up the past in my mind.

CHAPTER FIFTY-ONE
ANYWHERE BUT HERE ALL OVER AGAIN

It was two years since the death of my mother and one year since Emma's; I was still reeling from the consequences of losing Emma *and* my religion—struggling to create a new me.

I went for one last cup, but the coffee pot was full of dark, old grounds. *Sludge. That's exactly how I feel.* I couldn't offer the boys much more support that day. The trip to Jim's farm had left me fatigued, but they were running on adrenaline and wanted to shop for funeral clothes. I offered to tag along, but they said they'd go it alone. After a nap, I phoned Enos to see how he was doing. That phone conversation changed the way events would play out for my family. I dreaded having to tell my sons the shocking news.

When the boys returned, they were quietly subdued but also satisfied with their accomplishments. They emptied their shopping bags to display their selections.

"Wow," I said. "You guys have good taste."

"We got it from you," Jordan said with a smile.

"Plus, the salesclerks helped us," Jesse added.

"What did you buy, Jordan?" I asked.

"Nothing. Dad took Carolyn, Jonathan and me shopping a couple of weeks ago for dress clothes. He even bought a new suit for himself."

"Hmmm. That's convenient, I said."

"I was worried because I assumed they'd start back up to the meetings," Jordan said. "It's been a long time since they went to one. So I asked him why we were buying suits and shirts."

"And?"

"He said you never know when you'll need to go somewhere that requires dress clothes, and that it's best to be prepared."

All four of us exchanged knowing looks. We wondered if Jim had some kind of a premonition.

"We talked to Grandpa," Jason said. "There'll be an open casket because Dad's injuries don't prevent him from being shown."

"That's amazing!" I said. "I know you guys wanted to see Dad one more time."

"Can you take off work tomorrow and go with us to the visitation?"

Jordan said.

"Uh. Well, there's a problem with that."

"What problem? We need you," Jason said.

"And I need to be with you. But, Enos says Carolyn doesn't want me there."

"Who cares what she wants? You're our mother," Jordan said. "She can't tell you what to do."

"What's her deal, anyway?" Jason said.

"One of the neighbors saw me crying at their farm this morning," I said, "and when they told Carolyn she proceeded to go off her rocker. Enos warned me in no uncertain terms that I should stay away or else she will have me thrown out."

"Thrown out?" Jason said. "What the hell?"

None of us had considered this game-changing news bulletin. They were quite animated, no longer subdued, and quickly reached the point of resentment of their step-mother. They certainly didn't need this new emotion to deal with, but Carolyn had thrown it out into the arena.

"Let's all sit down and calmly talk about this." I said. We mulled over all of our options, and the three of them reached a unanimous decision: If I could not go, neither would they. This was a decision I could not abide, however.

"No!" I said. "You will regret it forever if you stay away from your father's funeral. The rest of the family needs your presence and, whether you guys realize it or not, you'll benefit from the family's encouragement. Remember the day Jim and Carolyn got married," I added, "and how we managed to convince Jordan to attend the wedding, even though he didn't want to?"

"I went because I had to," Jordan said. "It was the right thing to do."

"Precisely," I said. "Hold your heads up and be there for Dad and for each other."

Finally, Jesse said, "I don't see how she has any control over it."

"I'll see what I can find out. The last thing we want to do is add to the commotion, but I can't imagine not being there with you guys. Plus, I'd like to see Dad myself, one last time, to tell him goodbye."

I called the funeral home the next morning to see what my rights were. As it turned out, I had no rights whatsoever. At least that's the way it had been interpreted, although we found out later I had every right in the world to be there.

A man answered the phone. "Kraft Mortuary Services."

"Hello, I'm the mother of Jesse, Jason and Jordan Coe whose father is currently in your chapel."

"Yes. What can I do for you?"

"I'm hoping you can clarify something for me. I've been informed Jim's widow won't allow me to come to the funeral home with my sons, and I find that hard to believe. Do you know anything about it?"

"She has made her wishes known and we will honor them."

"How can you do that? My sons are grieving and especially distraught that I can't be with them."

"A funeral is like a private party. Whoever pays the bill can make up the invitation list, and you're not on it. If you *do* come and create a scene, we will call the police."

I laughed. "You'll call the *police?*"

"Just so you know."

Well.

"Sir, I realize you aren't familiar with me, and I have no idea what you've been told, but I assure you I am *not* a scene creator."

"I'm merely answering your question, Ma'am."

I took a deep breath. "Okay. Allow me to ask you one more. I was married to Jim for twenty-three years, and we had these three sons together and many good times through those years. I'd like to be able to get some closure for myself, even though I can't be there to support my children. Do you have any suggestions as to how I can do that?"

He paused. "You didn't hear this from me, but if you come very early in the morning before she arrives, don't announce yourself to our staff. Go directly into the chapel and say your goodbyes to your ex-husband quietly. If anyone reports your presence, we will be obligated to approach you and kindly request you leave." He paused. "Will that work for you?"

"It's better than nothing, I suppose, but I still don't understand why I'm being treated this way."

Mr. Kraft elaborated to my satisfaction: "This happens with some frequency, and it's nearly always the current wife who won't allow the ex-wife. From our experience, it appears the widow wants to be the only woman grieving. Of course, I have no idea whether or not that is true in this case, but it's an option you might consider to help you not take it so personally, even though it's difficult under the circumstances."

Up until then, I liked Carolyn. We had always been friendly, even having lunch together occasionally. I thought of what I'd learned about the survivor's behavior in the aftermath of death, running in circles out of control. The one thing she could control was me, and I comprehended that she wouldn't want me there, blubbering and sobbing like I'd done on her property the day before. In retrospect, I shouldn't have gone to the farm, but it was too late now. I couldn't imagine finding my husband mangled underneath bush-hog blades, but I knew for a certainty something had "snapped" inside her and I questioned if she would ever be able to work her way through the anguish. I assumed she would allow Jim's mother to be there, even though she would be grieving and crying too.

That evening, Jordan came home rejuvenated from all the support he'd received. "Some of the family said to tell you hi, and Aunt JoAnn knows what you must be going through. She thinks it's all wrong—the whole family thinks it's wrong, but there's nothing they can do to change Carolyn's mind."

"That's good to hear." I hadn't seen any of my former family since the day of the divorce.

"Dad looked like he was asleep, Mom. He looked good, considering. Do you think you'll go?"

"Probably not. I'd be uncomfortable walking in alone, and now that you've described Dad, I feel better. Will you tell him goodbye for me tomorrow?"

"I already did," Jordan said, smiling.

The next morning, I was getting ready for work and Jordan was playing a video game. He was the only family member who lived in Louisville, Kentucky. Everyone else, including the mortuary, was in Indiana, a twenty mile drive across the Ohio River.

"You should probably start getting dressed for the funeral. Who's picking you up?"

He offered a typical fifteen-year-old boy's shrug.

As the time came for me to leave for work, I called Jason but didn't get an answer. If he'd planned on transporting his brother he would've been here by now. I couldn't conscientiously go to the office and leave Jordan home alone unless I knew what the arrangements were.

"Do you think Carolyn took it for granted I would bring you to the funeral even though I'm not welcome?"

"Carolyn isn't thinking. She forgot about me already."

That did it. Something inside of me "snapped" just as had happened to Carolyn. You just don't casually "forget" your step-child at a time like this. At that exact moment I hated everyone in that family, even Jim. I'd be late for work, but it didn't matter. I told Jordan to hurry into my car. When we reached the funeral home, I felt a pang of guilt just pulling into the parking lot, but who else would bring Jim's son to his funeral if not for me? Still, my stomach was upside down and my knees had begun to shake, as though I feared the police were lying in wait for this intruder. I gathered my wits about me as best I could.

"I should go in, since I'm already here. Do you see any familiar cars in the parking lot?"

"No," Jordan said. "None that I recognize. I don't see Carolyn's car, but she probably isn't driving herself around.

"They still might make you leave, but if you want to come in with me," Jordan said, "I'll stay right by your side. You should tell Dad goodbye yourself and see him one last time."

"Are you sure?" I wouldn't risk putting Jordan in an uncomfortable situation if he didn't approve.

"It's your only chance. What have you got to lose?"

Fuck 'em all, I thought. *Why not? They forgot about Jim's son? I'm going in—I'll take my chances. Let them throw me out and call the police. I don't give a shit.*

He opened a leaded glass door and stood tall, walked me through like a gentleman. There were a few people in the room but I didn't recognize anyone. My knees were shaking worse than before.

We went straight for Jim, and Jordan placed his arm loosely around me. "Well . . . here he is," Jordan said proudly. He was right—no one would suspect the trauma Jim had suffered three days before. He'd been fitted with a heavy pullover sweater, and my first thought was that he would be uncomfortable on this hot August day. I wondered why Carolyn hadn't brought his new suit. Surely she wouldn't return it for a refund. Then, I realized how crazy this all sounded in my head. I took a deep breath, kept my emotions intact, and said goodbye to my first love.

From the corner of my eye I saw a man approaching quickly. I turned to leave, when the man grabbed my neck and shoulder with his large hand. I turned my head and recognized Bruce Grossman, an employee of Jim's I'd known for many years.

"You can't be here," Bruce growled.

"No? Well, I *am* here, but I'm just leaving. Get your hand off me." He didn't let go.

I pulled away from my attacker and Jordan grasped my arm. We walked casually to the front door where we hugged and I went on to work. I may as well have taken the day off, for all the good I was able to do in the office after that. My sons were at their dad's funeral, and I wasn't with them. I made several trips to the ladies room to cry undisturbed and unnoticed.

Jordan reported later that Grossman had followed us to the door, telling the funeral director not to let me back in. The funeral director said, "Who was that, the ex?"

162

Jordan glared at him and said, "*That*—is my mother!"

Grossman told Jordan he was sorry he had to do that. Jordan said, "You didn't *have* to do that. She only wanted to tell Dad goodbye."

Good ole Bruce Grossman. It didn't surprise me that he'd assumed it was his right to restrain me, the trespasser. I'd been Jim's bookkeeper when Bruce was hired. It hadn't taken long for Jim to peg him as a "brown-noser." Jim frequently called him "The Asshole" when he wasn't around. Jim's impressions of people were usually spot on and Bruce Grossman was no exception. Carolyn promoted him to Vice-President the following week. Think what you will about that.

Throughout the next few days, each of the boys shared tidbits of how they'd experienced their father's death and the mourning process with the family. I let them talk about it as long as they felt necessary. There would be years of grieving ahead for them, and for me.

Jordan's copy of the Last Will & Testament arrived by certified mail. We read it together and saw where a politically incorrect error had been made. Jim had signed his Will the day after our divorce, nine years previous. Thus, Carolyn was not mentioned as a part of his estate—only his three sons. Jim's Will specified all burial expenses would be paid by the estate. Jesse, Jason and Jordan *were* the estate, the ones who finally paid for this *private party*. They would have included me on the invitation list.

Oh well.

Even though Carolyn had assured Jason that Jim had left the boys a comfortable inheritance, and that she would not *contest* it, she wasted no time *electing* against Jim's will, claiming one-third of the inheritance. Jim and Carolyn had a multitude of jointly held business projects and assets. The house they lived in was hers, as well as the farm where Jim died. She was left with numerous funds of her own, but for some reason she wanted more so she took it from Jim's three sons, which caused them to wonder if she'd put on a show, married their dad for his money, then swiped a sizable chunk of what he'd left for them. I didn't know what to think.

I hired a lawyer to work with me to handle estate issues, as the Will called for me to be named Jordan's guardian. When I told the lawyer what had happened at the funeral home, he urged me to file suit in Criminal Court against Bruce Grossman for "unlawful touching" also known as Battery. Grossman had no authority to tell me to leave or to place his hand around my neck in a threatening manner. I had been in an auto accident a few months before and was undergoing physical therapy treatment for an injury. Grossman's rough grasp, and the quick turning of my head in response, had worsened the condition.

I thought seriously about taking action against him, but at the end of the day it wasn't worth it to embroil my family in further chaos. Enos still cleaned Jim's shop (now Carolyn's) on Fridays and Jesse worked there full-time as a machinist. They would surely suffer negative consequences from a court case. My family was of more importance to me than bringing "The Asshole" to his knees, although the thought of it was extremely tempting. Jordan and Jason urged me to do it; Jesse and Enos were against it. I decided to drop it.

I wondered when this insanity would ever end. Fortunately, Craig was in my life, standing strong beside me to serve as a cushion when I emotionally bounced off the walls, which was my daily routine for the next few months.`

CHAPTER FIFTY-TWO
REGAINED INNOCENCE

"Experience, which destroys innocence, also leads one back to it." ~James Arthur Baldwin, American Essayist, Playwright and Novelist, 1924-1987

When I left The Truth, I headed straight for the self-help department of my local bookstore, something JWs had always warned against. There was no end to the literature I found helpful. *The Power of Now* and *Conversations with God* were my favorites. My view of the entire human race evolved since I was no longer in a cult which put itself above and separate from it. I recognized a great diversity in the beliefs of the earth's population and the yin-yang balance cradled within. What a release it was to lose my lifelong fear of displeasing God.

Occasionally a JW stopped by to encourage me to return to the meetings. When I attempted to explain my new spiritual viewpoint, they turned their listening ears off. I read their facial expressions and body language: they pitied me, labeled me as an apostate, or someone from whom Jehovah had removed his approval. Their blinders were firmly attached.

"What about the future?" This was asked of me by someone who seemed sincerely interested in my chance of eternal life in a Paradise, or the loss of it. I was taken aback for a moment; I had forgotten how important the future was to those people.

What saddens me about this teaching, this way of thinking, is that the future—my tomorrow—will be *my* present day, but for them, many of whom I care deeply about, they will be on the "future treadmill" evermore. Such an eternal waste of a precious commodity—time. The present moment is all the *time* we have—it's so easy for me to see that now—and difficult to understand why others don't simply *know* it. My old friends have remained invisible and imaginary because of a time warp. I am in the present; they are living blindly, only for their future. That is their choice, of course, and it used to be mine.

~*~

Questions about life—and the answers. The Organization had them all, even though they wavered and changed periodically. How convenient—I knew it all by proxy. The negative results of this indoctrination were many. First and foremost, I did not develop the ability to think for myself, to make my own decisions, to research and question. I naively accepted whatever information was handed down from the *Wise Sages of New York*, because, after all, they said it was from Jehovah God.

Secondly, even now, after all of these years, when I am in public, I often feel as though I don't belong; I am a nobody—the after-effects of living within parenthetical brackets—remove me from a sentence and no one will notice.

I worked with a therapist regarding my confusion over Emma's death and the holocaust which followed. My perspective slowly changed.

"What a surprise for me," I said, "when on one single day, nearly all the true friends I'd accumulated through the years turned out to be not at all what I'd imagined."

"Is that *really* what happened?" she said in a tone of voice which told me she didn't believe it.

"It *felt* like it. Do you see it differently?"

She explained, "*You're* the one who didn't live up to *their* expectations."

I relaxed at the realization of the truth in her words. "You're so right! I'm the one who changed; I turned out to be not what they'd imagined."

"And good for you; you took a quantum leap! Not just everyone will summon the courage it takes."

Yet, even with that new viewpoint, I couldn't seem to get comfortable in my chair, loathe to admit and genuinely embarrassed to think that I was, at the age of fifty, unsure about the existence of God. I attempted to explain my humiliation. "That is to say . . . um . . . most people ponder these questions much earlier in life, don't they?"

Her response surprised me. "Perhaps many never ask these questions at all."

"But . . . why would one not?"

She shrugged and said, "Because they don't feel a need to know everything."

Did *I* really need to know? I wondered. My inquiries as a five-year-old had landed me in a highly-controlled cult. Perhaps I should back away from seeking enlightenment of any kind. And yet, up until then, I believed that innocent, simplistic thinking made one inferior. In fact, I was quite touchy about it—even a tiny bit paranoid—and overly sensitive to think I no longer knew it all, as I'd thought. Could I discover a comfortable middle-ground spiritually?

During the next three years, Craig good-naturedly listened while I described the details of my JW history. He pointed out controlling tendencies in most religions, especially Christianity. But wait! I was a Christian. Or was I? Was I an old sweater with a little girl's name tag sewn in by a loving mother? The girl grew up and donated her sweater to charity, but the tattered label was still intact—a label which no longer applied.

While feverishly searching for answers, I met a holistic psychologist who held small workshops in her home, gatherings where I learned the usefulness of energy work. I made new friends, like-minded people who had found inner peace, or were hoping to master it. Our hostess provided a Zen atmosphere, emphasizing experiential wisdom in the attainment of enlightenment, de-emphasizing theological knowledge in favor of direct self-realization through the use of meditation. We attended a "Monk's Walk" where we wore hooded robes and remained silent during an entire weekend, speaking only during group meetings. Craig graciously accompanied me, curious to see how I could possibly go an entire weekend without talking! We walked a labyrinth and were shown how to center, focus on the present moment. Recall, I'd never had to draw on my inner resources. This was all new to me—the present—I'd been racking up mileage on the "future treadmill" for most of my life.

I chose to name this chapter "Retained Innocence" because during the period of two or three years of extensive reading, seeking and self-reasoning, I finally learned to accept my down-to-earth-ness, my undemanding innocence.

I adopted a Zen approach, living in the moment, finding inner peace as I'd never experienced it before. I had never known such spiritual contentment within the confines of religion. There were days I felt so joyful I wanted to announce to the world that I'd found the real meaning of life!

One of my preferred quotes is from Abraham-Hicks: "It doesn't really matter what religion anybody believes. If their life is working (and there are many different approaches to life that are working very well) then why not let them believe whatever they want to believe? It's all working in the way that it is supposed to be. There are religions that you wouldn't want anything to do with, that are perfect mechanisms for the people who are involved in them. And therefore, they are a very good thing."

On my road to a healthy spiritual state, religion had become an obstacle, so I maneuvered around and away from it. I have found that making peace with where I am is easier when I've made peace with where everyone else is, even those who choose not to associate with me any longer. I am where I'm *supposed* to be.

CHAPTER FIFTY-THREE
MEDITATION IN THE MEDICATION ROOM

While I'd had no interest in another marriage, and certainly no self-imposed religious or moral reason to rush into another one, three years after Craig and I met, we decided to marry barefooted on St. Augustine Beach on June 6, 2001, with all six of our grown children beside us and my three-year-old granddaughter tossing rose petals onto the sun-baked sand. The fact that I'd been baptized on June 6 was a coincidence, but this commitment was just as important to me. I discovered later that my mother's parents were married on June 6, and my mother had graduated from Arsenal Technical High School in Indianapolis on that date.

Craig and I had taken a trip to Grand Cayman the year before, where Craig had proposed on the balcony of our vacation condo overlooking the majestic North Sound. He did not use the "M" word in his proposal. It was more like, "Would you spend the rest of your life with me?" I said yes, but I wasn't sure if he meant marriage. He took my hand and slid a ring on, a little too loose, but I wore it anyway. We would have it resized at home.

We'd brought a copy of the Tom Cruise and Gene Hackman film, "*The Firm*," to find the exact locations of the scenes shot there on the island. The phone booth near Avery's Boat Rental where Hackman had made a crucial call was the first one we located. We squeezed into it and Craig asked for his ring back. He wanted to elaborate on his proposal. He added his hope of our life together being a happy one, and how we would support one another through the good and the bad. Still no "M" word. I agreed and the ring went back on. We walked through the downtown area, a typical cruise port with expensive jewelry stores such as Cartier. Inside, we found the perfect wedding ring, a narrow, squared, white-gold "tank" style with one channel-set diamond. We were astonished at how perfectly it matched my engagement ring. Our budget wouldn't accommodate a Cartier diamond, but we took a brochure with us.

We hadn't set a wedding date, as there had been no mention of marriage, but it was obvious that's what he had in mind, if only he could say the word. He borrowed my ring again at the famous Blow Holes and at the Hyatt open-air bar where we ordered tropical drinks, just as Hackman and Cruise had done. Craig proposed a total of seven times in separate locations on the island that week, and on each occasion he expounded on what our lives would be like together, the plans he had for our future, and how we would meld our families. Finally, we went to Hell and back—Hell, Grand Cayman, that is. It had become second nature for me to remove my ring by then, so I handed it to him, but he backed off and said, "There's no way I'm proposing in Hell. That would conjure up some bad juju for sure!" We laughed at the comedy we'd created. I wondered if he realized he hadn't actually said, "Will you marry me?" Semantics—since I'd grown up in an organization that placed so much importance on exact and proper words, I had my heart set on hearing the "M" word.

The following month, we took a Memorial Day weekend trip to visit my cousin, Tracey, and her fiancé. Their spectacular lake home in Miller Beach, Indiana, had the perfect view of the Chicago skyline.

Craig and I spent one day by ourselves as tourists. We shopped our way down Michigan Avenue where a Cartier store jumped out at us. We rang the doorbell. A salesman, dressed like a proper butler, let us in and we found the tank ring identical to the one in Grand Cayman, and it was in my exact size! I could see the gears in Craig's brain turning, but we still hadn't set a wedding date. He told the salesman we'd be back. I imagined the guy thinking, *Yeah right, I'm sure you will.*

We headed north to the city of Mundelein where Craig had grown up. We toured his favorite haunts: a bowling alley and a pizza joint, ending at the park close to his childhood home. In that park, he said he'd decided to go back to Cartier and buy the ring.

"It's a wedding ring you know," I said, "but you haven't asked me to marry you." Craig's face took on a shocked expression. "What I mean to say is that you haven't actually used the 'M' word, so I wonder if marriage is really what you want." He'd been divorced twice, so maybe he was just as afraid of commitment as I was. I was, without a doubt, anxious about doing it a fourth time.

Craig scratched his head and appeared to be reminiscing about our week in Grand Cayman. He put his arms around me and said, "I love you and want to marry you. Will you *please* marry me?"

"Well, since you put it that way, of course I will," I said. "All you had to do was ask."

"I thought I'd done that a few times already," Craig mumbled. "Apparently my *husband training* isn't complete." He took my hand and we headed for Chicago and the Magnificent Mile, where he bought my ring and had it shipped to his home in Indiana. At last, we started a dialog about our wedding—when and where, etc.

A couple of weeks later, a banging noise sounded at my front door.

There stood Craig holding a bulky twenty-seven inch television. He walked in like he owned the place and carried it down the hallway. "I figure since I'm going to be moving in, I should bring some of my things."

I blinked and remained speechless. We hadn't discussed the timing of his move-in, and I hadn't expected this. Furthermore, I'd never known a man to place more importance on a television than his clothes or toiletries.

He set the monstrosity on a large storage trunk in the already over-crowded master bedroom and plugged it in. Craig obviously thought a TV in the bedroom was normal, but I'd never wanted one. In fact, I hadn't been a fan of television ever since cable took over with fifty channels of nothing good to watch. During the day, when Craig was at work, I stared at the vast blackness of the screen and the world's largest eyesore stared right back at me.

Craig put his house up for sale and moved more of his personal belongings into my place. Soon, it was *our* place. But there was another problem. Craig had cats. He'd had one of his own, Ginger, a short-haired cat. He'd inherited another when his mother went into a nursing home. When his two youngest children asked if he would take theirs because their mother had developed an allergy to them, he couldn't refuse. Somehow, another cat was added to the mix, making five. Whenever I spent any time at Craig's house, I'd start itching within an hour. I'd developed an allergy to the long-haired felines. I wasn't sure what could be done about that, and my apartment was so small there was no practical place for a litter box, but I asked him to bring Ginger and see how it worked out. Craig, however, made the decision to become pet-free. Eventually, and with much effort, he found good homes for all five.

Most of the other adjustments we needed to make were accomplished during the next few months, the first being that he set the timer on the television so it wouldn't stay on all night. I couldn't sleep with a variety of voices, weird music and applause floating around our room, not to mention the flickering light. Usually, he fell fast asleep within five minutes and I used the remote to turn the contraption off. Craig, his television, and I lived together for one year before our beach wedding.

Craig soon grew tired of cramped apartment living, especially in a space where he had no control over the HVAC system. We searched for property back in Indiana close to Enos, now eighty-eight, and found a four-acre lot just down the road that we were prepared to make an offer on. But, one day, after I'd pulled into Enos' driveway, I looked next door longingly at my old home, as usual, and what did I see but a *For Sale* sign! First, I called the realtor from my cell phone. Next, I called Craig.

"Have you been praying to God for a sign?"

"Huh? Not that I know of," Craig said, laughing.

"Well, there's a sign in the front yard next to Enos, and the adorable house I built in the two-acre woods is back on the market!"

"Holy Moly," Craig said. "How much are they asking?"

"Too much."

"Okay. Let's take a look at it!" Craig was fully aware of my "Leap and the net will appear" philosophy. The house would be ours!

After some negotiation, we bought it in October, 2002. Enos stood by on moving day while I directed the movers as to furniture placement, and I recalled the last time I'd seen him grin so widely—the day he married my mother. I wondered if his happiness hinged on a misguided hope that I would find my way to the meetings now that I was back in my home, but he never mentioned it again. He was truly happy to have us as neighbors. And Craig, well . . . he's been fixing my thermostats ever since! He installed a new one in our home last month, and he programmed it just for me and my ups and downs. He knows me that well.

One beautiful day, I found my own Paradise when I turned one room of our home into what I think of as The Meditation Room. Jason calls it Mom's *Medication* Room, but isn't he the very one who wanted to be part of a cowboy and Indian team when he grew up? He actually believes he's a pirate at this stage.

My special room has a sliding glass patio door where I look out over the woods and search for answers from within. I could have done that a long time ago if I had thought of it, but I'd been taught it was necessary to look outside, heavenward, for God. How delighted I was to discover my very own answers! The tools I used were my heart, my conscience and my common sense. After all, don't believers of all religions consider those to be God-given gifts: the heart, conscience and common sense? If we weren't meant to use them, why else would they have been given to us?

I reach and nearly touch the trees from my patio door, especially when the leaves are orange, red and yellow. Early in the morning is a special time for me to be there in the stillness; appreciating the beauty of the Earth; the deer living in the woods; the birds' morning music; an occasional puff of white clouds in a clear sky; and the quiet of the countryside. I've become a tree-hugger who does not worship a god, but I'm not worried. If there really is a god who made the trees, when I hug one isn't it the same as worship anyway?

In the end, I believe appreciation is of much more value than worship. It's all semantics. You know that by now, right?

CHAPTER FIFTY-FOUR
HYPOCROCISY ABOUNDS

Six months after we'd moved back into the home I'd been so lucky to have re-obtained, Jason walked over to visit Enos. He immediately ran back home. "You'd better hurry over there—he's talking in complete sentences but he's not making any sense." I called an ambulance and we rushed to the local hospital where they discovered lung and brain cancer. Enos was eighty-eight and one-half years old. He died exactly thirty days later.

While he was in the hospital, many of Enos' friends from the congregation stopped by to visit him. Some brought cards and chocolates. I found it odd, though, that during the twenty days he was there, only one plant arrived: a large, potted Schefflera. The bland environment of his room, "decorated" with white walls, ceiling, bed-linens and a plain grey linoleum floor was not at all like home, where he'd nurtured a large collection of greenery on a plant shelf near the front window of his living room. I'd assumed some of the congregation members, or even his family from afar, would send something to make his hospital stay bright and cheerful. I'd made sure the florist delivered the Schefflera the day after he was admitted, but it sat all alone for nearly three weeks.

I visited Enos for an hour or two every day. On one of those occasions, he offered me a chocolate. I opened the box and saw quite a few were already missing. I smiled. My generous step-dad, playing host to his friends, offering them refreshment even while on his death bed. We had visited for about five minutes and I said, "The Schefflera plant is sure doing nicely there by the window, isn't it?"

He nodded. "It's from Rebecca." His face sported a hearty grin.

I smiled and laughed slightly. "That was so sweet of her," I said. I didn't remind him it was from me, because I saw the pleasure it brought him to think his niece had sent it. But on another occasion, he told me it had come from the Lowland Congregation and it took everything I had to keep Dainy, my still ever-present imaginary friend, from resurfacing! Old age and brain cancer—not a good mixture, I told her, so let it be. Whatever his imagination conjured up to keep him happy was fine with me.

One day, while he was sleeping, I sat beside his bed and glanced through the cards. A message: *Call if you need anything. Get well soon,* was written on nearly every card. I wondered if they were all in denial—*Get well soon?*

Enos didn't want to die in the sterile environment of the hospital, but he required continuous care. Even though I lived next door, I still worked in Louisville three days a week, and to bring him back to his own comfy bedroom would require a lot of assistance from others. So, I asked the congregation elders to please put out a request to some of these well-meaning friends to lend me a hand. Enos Kimball was a long-time elder and a pioneer with the Lowland Congregation, and in such a case it was customary for an elder or ministerial servant to prepare a list of volunteers who would take shifts caring for the patient's physical needs. When I inquired three days later of the elder to whom I'd spoken previously, he rationalized that no list had been prepared for Enos' case because he hadn't had time to do it. He said he'd mention it to a few people.

His wife rang me up later to ask if I was disfellowshipped. I am not disfellowshipped, and I haven't committed a sin that would be unforgivable, unless writing this book falls into that category. I didn't fall into a life of debauchery, develop an adulterous lifestyle, smoke cigarettes, cheat, steal or lie. I assured her I was not disfellowshipped, but I was curious as to why she'd inquired. She explained some of the sisters had wondered, as though they would be helping *me* and not Enos. It was their dear elder and pioneer brother who wanted to die at home; *he* needed their assistance and I assumed they would've put their own business aside to aid him in that objective. But, because *I* had left The Truth, even though I wasn't officially cast out, they evidently wanted no part of helping me care for Enos. She asked if his toileting would be part of the "job" at hand. I said of course it would. She brainlessly told me she couldn't do such a thing, to expose an elder's private parts!

Unbelievable! I silently counted to ten, practicing forbearance. "We're all naked under our clothes," I said. "His being an elder should be reason enough for you to want to do anything to keep him comfortable during these last of his days." She never called back. One sister offered assistance, Gertie Griffin, a lady I had always admired. She was seventy-two and recovering from rotator cuff surgery. She said she was unable to lift anything heavy, but she'd be glad to help any way she could. Heavy lifting, of Enos, was what I needed the most. I thanked her for her call; surely others would follow.

~*~

I had him brought home, assuming help was on the way. After twenty four hours, I realized I'd made a crucial mistake. I couldn't handle it, physically or emotionally. I was only one person, yet I needed a team. Back to the hospital Enos went until I could figure it all out. When the ambulance pulled out of his driveway after his one night at home, one of the attendants asked him what his problem was. "Old age of the brain," Enos said.

I sat on his back porch and sobbed, broken in half to see him leave his home for the last time. I had an extremely urgent desire to call my long-time, go-to elder Brother Graham. I hadn't seen or talked to him for a long time, but I wanted to share my grief and frustration with the inability to care for my step-dad by myself, without any assistance from congregation members. I knew Graham would listen and understand. I didn't call him—I merely sat there on the steps and thought intensely about whether or not I should. Within five minutes he pulled into the driveway. I couldn't believe my eyes! He looked like an angel.

"I was just wishing you were here." I sobbed.

"I got here as fast as I could," he said with a smile and a hug. "It's really odd," he said, scratching his head. "I had no intention of stopping by, but I was running errands when the thought occurred to me out of the blue, so I detoured from my route and here I am! We talked for awhile and, as per usual, he brought comfort to me.

I was about to panic when Hospice stepped in for the essentials, but I was left with no other choice than to admit Enos to a private nursing facility for twenty-four hour care during his final days. I didn't know how much time he had left, or if he would comprehend the move out of the hospital. I considered not even mentioning that he wouldn't be able to go home again. Was it possible he wouldn't notice? Honesty was the route I chose; when I explained the situation, his expression saddened because he was still alert enough to realize he would never again experience comfort from within his own bedroom.

Enos had a lift-recliner, a special chair he dearly loved, given to him as a gift by an elder. I had it delivered to the nursing facility. He used it every day he was there, which turned out to be about ten days. Ten days was all the time anyone from Enos' congregation would have had to donate their precious time to help Enos die at home, his last wish.

I was with him when he passed, holding his hand and softly talking to him. It's much different than the excitement one feels at the birth of a baby. Just like birth, death is a natural part of life, and the ability to witness it with one I loved was a calming experience I'd never known possible. I'd felt it with my mother, too.

After Enos died, I donated his lift-recliner to the nursing home and gave his Chevy and many household items to Hospice. The elder who'd given the chair to Enos, the same one who hadn't taken the time to prepare a list of volunteers, the man whose wife didn't want to assist Enos with toileting, threw me a look of annoyance when he realized I'd not brought the recliner back after Enos died. *Back to where?* I wondered. He said others in the congregation had wanted to use it.

"I see. Well, if anyone had cared to communicate that fact with me beforehand, I would have been happy to oblige," I said. "Communication comes in handy that way."

"Yes, well, I told Enos when he was in the hospital we'd let Brother 'So and So' use it, and Enos agreed," the elder explained, wagging his head in a superior manner. I fought the urge to slap him.

Now it was my turn to look annoyed. "Sorry. He never told me. You did realize he had brain cancer, right?" I didn't wait around for his answer. Who in their right mind believes anything they say to an aged man, dying from brain cancer, will be repeated to the person responsible for doing the work later on?

Craig and I were delighted the facility we'd found to take care of Enos would use the recliner for their other terminal patients. They had been paid to do what Enos' Christian brothers and sisters refused to do—fulfill their Christian obligation to care for one another. I thought of the nursery rhyme, The Little Red Hen. She asked everyone to help her bake bread, but they all had excuses as to why they couldn't. When the bread came out of the oven, hot and aromatic, everyone wanted a piece. Too bad for them, said the Little Red Hen.

~*~

Enos had pre-arranged his funeral. I was to present a small portion of the Memorial Service—five minutes describing the joy of having Enos as a family member; Jordan was to offer a lively five-minute description of Enos' childhood, as he had interviewed Enos with a cassette tape-recorder the year before in preparation for a book he planned to write about our family tree; and lastly, Doug Kimball, Enos' nephew and an elder, would give a twenty-minute Bible talk. The Organization made it clear that an elder was never to share a religious funeral with another religious belief, such as a multi-denominational service.

Brother Graham told me that if I'd chosen him to give the spiritual portion of the service, he wouldn't have agreed to do it.

"Well . . . I didn't ask you, now did I? So you don't have to worry about it. Enos wanted a *family* service and Doug is his nephew so it all works out fine." Brother Graham warned me some congregation members weren't planning to attend because they were unsure whether or not Enos would actually have a Witness funeral. No one called to inquire about the plans, or whether I needed any assistance, etc., but the gossip was buzzing so loud I could practically feel it. I was the executor of my step-father's estate; my love for him would not have allowed me to have any kind of service but a Witness one! It promised to be a refreshingly unique and delightful Memorial Service held on Mother's Day. Since Witnesses don't observe that occasion, I selected that day for the convenience of out-of-town JW family who would make the one-hundred mile trip and back.

Visitation would start at noon and the short program was to be at 4 PM. I awakened early that morning to write my little presentation. The only thing left was to eat breakfast and change clothes, but I had no desire for food and could barely concentrate—uneasy and tense when I thought of standing up in front of all those Jehovah's Witnesses who were no longer my close friends . . . people I had known well who would be in the audience, judging me silently, wondering what worldly things I'd been up to since I'd left the flock.

I took a royal blue silk suit out of the closet and laid it on my bed, with matching antique blue glass earrings placed next to it. Now, with dress shoes on the floor, the outfit was ready to go, but there was no one inside. Everyone else in the family was dressed and ready. The anxiety mounted immensely, and I procrastinated to the point of running late, as though I could delay the inevitable. The outfit lay there, beckoning, calling my name. I couldn't recall the last time I'd felt such dread. Once I was dressed up, I'd have to make my way to the funeral home; but if I weren't dressed, well, then I couldn't go. I'd put it on hold forever.

The phone rang. My cousin Tracey was calling. "How are you doing?" she said.

"Not too well. I can't get dressed."

"Why not?"

"It's weird, but I can't seem to take my pajamas off."

"Oh." She paused for a moment. "Wouldn't you do it anyway? I mean, if there were no funeral today, wouldn't you have changed clothes without even thinking about it?

"Of course. But this is different."

"It's only a speed bump, cousin. You've been jumping through J-Dub hoops all your life; surely you can make it over this last hurdle and erase them from your life for once and for all."

She'd sensed what I hadn't yet grasped: the simple act of dressing up had caused an unrealistic anxiety, making a chore out of it as though I'd never done it before. Geez, I'd changed outfits every day of my life, so what was the big deal about that day? Tracey and I shared laughter about my predicament and the dread instantly disappeared. Confidence fully restored, I slipped into my suit, applied blush, non-toxic blue eye-shadow, and jewelry, checked out my appearance in a full-length mirror and went to the funeral home.

Doug Kimball had told Jordan and me to write what we wanted to say and Doug would read it to the audience. I discounted his plan, for it was Enos' wish that we participate personally. I told him he didn't have to participate if he was uncomfortable doing so, although Enos had specifically asked for him. Doug reluctantly agreed, but wanted us to e-mail our copies to him. I didn't do it since I hadn't written it until that very morning; otherwise I would've been happy to accommodate him. We had only two days from when Enos died to the funeral, and there were way too many details to take care of than to worry about satisfying the nitpicking needs of an elder. Even though Doug was a really nice guy, he was a marionette puppet and I knew who held his strings.

Once we arrived, Doug called us aside. *Here it comes,* I thought. We seated ourselves at a small round table and he asked to review our prepared orations. Doug removed a pen authoritatively from his shirt pocket and crossed out words such as *eulogy, missionary* and *karma.* Doug said these were inappropriate, not Bible-based expressions if applied incorrectly. (Incorrectly, according to The Organization, he meant.)

"In other words," I said, "since *you* are covering the Bible portion of the service, you don't want *us* to use terminology that would refer to anything spiritual?"

"Right, and if you insist on using these words during your presentations, I couldn't possibly follow-through by giving my portion of the memorial service."

Semantics again, and more game-playing, I thought. *When will it ever end?*

Jordan and I looked at one another and rolled our eyes when Doug wasn't looking. We assured him there would be no problem. A wave of nausea passed through me and I took a deep breath. I knew this would be the very last time I would *ever* allow myself to be in a position where the Organization could dictate my behavior, remove a word from my mouth or insert another. I've wondered what would've been the outcome if I said "karma" like I'd originally planned. Doug had been emphatic about that

177

particular phrase because it applies to Hinduism or Buddhism and was not a Christian expression. Would he *really* refuse to honor his uncle with a scriptural discourse? How disrespectful and awkward would that have been? Jordan and I did not even consider allowing the possibility of it.

Afterward, Brother Graham and his wife stood and left the chapel immediately. My stomach did a flip-flop; had our family presentations been that offensive? Apparently not, for the remainder of the audience formed a line and offered expressions of appreciation to Jordan and me for our unique viewpoints. They were delighted to learn that Enos had a tendency to fight older boys as a youngster, and how his mother sewed a cut on his forehead as he lay bravely on the wooden kitchen table after falling out of a tree. They enjoyed the visualization during my description of our beloved, five-foot, four-inch Enos transporting an extremely large video camera on his shoulder all throughout Disney World, recording our family vacation in 1986.

Enos' niece, Rebecca, pulled me aside. "I knew what Jim told me couldn't be true. I've known you a long time and watched the way you took care of Enos. Jim said you'd sent little Jordan to Jim's wedding with dirty ripped pants. I *knew* you wouldn't have done that."

I shook my head and laughed. "Thanks for telling me. From what I understand, Jim was famous for slander back in that period of his life. Truthfully, that's the way he sent Jordan home, not the way I sent him there, not that it matters anymore."

The next day, Brother Graham called to say how much he had enjoyed all three parts of Enos' Memorial Service. They'd had an appointment which caused them to leave abruptly, but he wanted to let me know he was proud of me, after all.

At the funeral home, what did the Lowland Congregation provide for Enos' friends and family to eat? Over one-hundred people made the trip (the majority were Jehovah's Witnesses), undoubtedly expecting some type of nourishment before going home. I, myself, was famished after the entire affair. Oh, but wait! I found the funeral home's kitchen to be devoid of anything edible. Clean as a whistle, as they say—only a hand-written paper sign, "Enos Kimball," sat alone and deserted on the countertop. I broke into tears and wadded it up, threw it into the nearest waste can. Enos' congregation had already thrown him into the trash. Never had I experienced a Witness funeral where casseroles and desserts weren't donated in abundance. Even meatloaves would've been welcomed! I hadn't thought it would be necessary for me to ask congregation members to provide for Enos' final visitors, as that had always been an automatic response to the death of a congregation member.

The funeral director, Nancy Kraft, said of all the Jehovah's Witness funerals she'd overseen, (dozens of them through the years) this was the only one she could remember where no food had been brought in. She had assumed we were all going out to a restaurant, which is what his relatives were eventually forced to do.

I went home, drank a cup of warm milk, climbed back into my pajamas and went straight to bed—I'd lost my appetite. One word floated through my consciousness as I drifted off: *disrespect*. Then, nearly in a dream state, I clarified it to read *second-hand* disrespect. I relaxed and fell asleep, satisfied with the knowledge I'd done my very best to care for him the past seven years.

I was glad Enos was sleeping, waiting for his resurrection. I wouldn't have wanted him to see such cold, calculated and selfish behavior from God's only true followers. Apparently, Enos had unwittingly collected a few imaginary friends of his own.

CHAPTER FIFTY-FIVE
BLINDERS 0FF—BLINDERS ON

*"Any entity worthy of being called a god would be above it all and would probably care more about how kind you were to others, and whether you left the world just a little bit better." Anu Garg (*www.Wordsmith.org*)*

While growing up, I saw my religion as a straightforward and simple one to follow. The Organization seemed harmless at first glance but was, and is, anything *but* innocent. At long last I have the freedom to choose my beliefs. I positively believe I'm more content living in a world among millions of people who don't have all the answers than trapped within parentheses with a few hundred-thousand know-it-alls.

There are days when I reapply my blinders on purpose, to focus on what is really important to me now. I don't want the distraction of residual memories of my religion-induced behaviors, nor do I need the influence of others' beliefs to find happiness. I realize people mean well, but frankly I tire of offers of people insisting I try *their* church, as though I need a church at all! They just don't *get* it.

No. No. No. I don't need one. I don't want one. The only service I might enjoy, for the powerful musical experience alone, would be in a church which houses a massive pipe organ. I sometimes blast the Hallelujah Chorus at full volume from my Infinity floor speakers and Bose Surround Sound which makes for one astounding spiritual event in my very own living room, with its hardwood floor, tall cathedral ceiling and wall-to-wall windows. It's just like the real thing. Let me rephrase: It *is* the real thing. It's my way to show *appreciation* for the earth's beauty right outside, mixed with the glory of music—the organ, trumpet and the human voice.

Forty-five years of one's life is a large chunk of time, and as much as I'd like to simply forget it, I can't. It shaped me, formed me, and greatly influenced my personality. So, ever-so-often, blinders enable me to put it all behind and live in the present moment with the happiness and freedom I found in my Meditation Room and beyond.

Just like my non-existent bumper sticker, I'm an ambivalent non-believer, if one must put a label on me.

While I am now a part of the world, I was brain-trained not to be, to keep myself *separate* from the world inside of parenthetical brackets. I'm not worldly in the most common sense of the word. I accessorize well and with the use of "smoke and mirrors" can appear equally as smart and classy as the next girl on any given occasion, but I harbor a nagging hint of inadequacy. It's hard to pinpoint an exact definition because it's wispy, translucent, a residual guilt, as though I'm doing something I shouldn't. I vote in political elections, stand with pride while singing the National Anthem, and I play a collection of patriotic music from the CD player of my car, at full volume with the garage doors open, while my grown sons set off fireworks in our back yard on the Fourth of July.

I share my happiness and celebrate holidays now with my family and true friends. We conduct our daily affairs of life without religious guilt, but with that ever-desired *gusto!* I celebrated Christmas for the first time as an adult in 1998, the year Jim died. Every subsequent year, I second-guess my reasons for putting up and decorating my Christmas tree, as though everything I do needs a specific reason, a concept ingrained in me early on. Why would an ambivalent non-believer celebrate a religious holiday? Craig reminds me I'm decorating the tree with my grandchildren for fun, family, and for the memories it will leave with them. And it *is* fun, there's no doubt. But, I wonder if Jehovah's Witnesses will see my blinking pink tree lights while driving past. Will they judge, shake their heads in disgust and disappointment, seeing firsthand how low I have stooped? (The first two years I closed my mini-blinds at night so the tree couldn't be seen from the road.)

Should and shouldn't are harsh, unnecessary words, in my newly altered opinion. I use the "semantic technique" for different phraseology, word substitutions so my behavior and thoughts aren't being judged, as though a Higher Power up above is going to send that infamous lightning bolt down any second! I wrote previously that I've removed the word "should" from my vocabulary, but I find it lingers in my conscience. For example, I experience a subtle guilt when I watch an R-rated movie with foul language. And yet, what happens when I drop and break an egg on the floor? "Fuck," I say. Sometimes I say it repeatedly before cleaning up the mess. Once I did that—said "fuck, fuck, fuck!"—not realizing both of my grandchildren were in their toy-room at the rear of my house. I'd thought they were playing outside. They scampered up the hallway into the kitchen, bright-eyed, with their little hands covering joyful giggles trickling from their mouths. "MaMoo!" they gasped and squealed. My mouth fell open and my eyes widened at the shock of what I'd done. Greta nodded and smiled knowingly, one eyebrow raised as if to say, "Yep, we heard it all." (They occasionally remind me of that day.)

CHAPTER FIFTY-SIX
MT. WASHINGTON CEMETERY

I've kept in touch with Emma's mother, Lydia, now a typical grandmother. She shows me pictures of Emma's sons and brags about how they've grown up physically and spiritually in the Organization. They see their father occasionally, but were largely raised by Emma's parents after her death. Anthony is married and has a child of his own. I smile when I think of Emma as a grandmother! I would've liked to have remained a part of the boys' lives, but relentless emotional pain held me back. I had foreseen a time when they would be discouraged from associating with me, as I had walked away from The Truth. In so doing, I gave up my chance to share tasty tidbits about the delicious friendship their mother had with JoEmma. They each have memories, of course, but they don't have mine. Perhaps I will send them a copy of this book with an invitation for them to contact me.

While working on my rewrites and final edits, I developed a strong desire to visit Emma's grave which had been moved years ago. Thanks to Lydia's directions, I found it. She offered to go with me, but this was something I wanted to do alone.

The fact that I visited the grave is just that, a fact, the honest truth. The conversation Emma and I had there is entirely fiction, of course. When two people know each other as well as Emma and I did, they can discern what their friend would think or say on any number of given subjects. So, I put the words in her mouth. Since we'd always finished one another's sentences, I didn't think it would be wrong to do so. If anyone has a problem with it, they can write their own version of the conversation. After all, isn't that what Aiden Munroe did? And he got by with it, too.

Lydia had told me there would be no bench to sit on, so I brought a blanket for the ground, folded it in half and sat down.

"It's about time you showed up here, JoEmma," Emma said.

"Sorry about that. I'm not sure what's kept me," I said.

"You've been busy writing."

"That I have," I agreed.

"I heard you say goodbye to me the day before I died. Did you know?"

"Really? I'd hoped you did, but I had no way of knowing. It's not like you were in any condition to give me a sign."

"Oh yeah, I heard everybody, believe you me. I thought they would *never* quit singing. You were there—you know what I'm talking about. My God, most of them were way off key!"

I'd gone to Emma's grave with a box of Kleenex, thoroughly expecting to cry, but here she had me crying with laughter!

"I showed up real early on Sunday morning," I said. "Thomas met me at the elevator. He said you'd just passed away . . . I was too late."

"It's okay. I thought I'd better high-tail it out of there before the Glee Club showed up again."

"Can't say as I blame you," I said. "Bryan and Nate were already there. I guess they'd spent the night. Anyway, I sat with you for awhile until it was time to let you go, but Nate wouldn't leave your side."

"That's nice to know," Emma said. "Nate always did have a real soft spot."

"Finally, Bryan told me to go in there and make Nate leave because the guys from the morgue had shown up and they wanted to move your body to the funeral home. I'm not sure why Bryan thought I could influence Nate to do anything . . . but it worked. I sat down beside him, next to your body, and we talked about old times. He told me he'd promised to take Joey and Anthony to the beach for a vacation after it was all over. I'm pretty sure he did, too.

"When Nate finally moved into the empty room next to yours with the rest of the family, I waited in the hallway for them to wheel you out. I couldn't believe my eyes—you were zipped inside a black body bag!"

"Come again?"

"I know, right? I mean, I figured you'd be covered with a white sheet like in the movies, but, no, you were in a body bag of all things. I thought I'd faint."

"Well, of all the nerve!" Emma said.

"I stood there, dumbfounded, and watched as two attendants transferred you into the elevator, knowing my best friend was inside of the bag. I knew I'd never see you again since you were to be cremated. Bryan came up behind me and took my hand, told me to come on into the other room with everyone else. He said there was nothing I could do for you now and I didn't need to see anymore."

"He always was the smart one in the family," Emma giggled with a little snort, like she used to.

Finally, I brought up the painful subject. "Emma, if I'd known you were bothered by my comments in that phone call, I would've set your mind at ease. I wish you'd given me the chance. I was devastated to find out you'd died and had been upset with me."

"Oh snap! I wasn't the least bit upset with you. That lame girl liked to stir up trouble. You know how she was. I think she wanted Thomas for herself, personally. All I'd said was you had a casual attitude about remarriage, and I'd told you that the day we talked. We had different viewpoints, that's all, which was unusual for us, but you had the right to feel the way you did. I knew you had no interest in going after Thomas. I wish you had, come to think of it, 'cause he'd be a far sight better off than he is now."

"Well, I don't know about that. I haven't seen him, but your mom said he never remarried since you made him promise he wouldn't."

"Don't remind me," Emma said.

"Okay, but, I still would've liked the chance to talk it over with you, to not leave it hanging."

"You remember what my mother said to you?"

"You were sick and not always in your right mind, so not to pay any attention to what you did or didn't do toward the end."

"Well," Emma said, "there you go, then."

"But why did you keep so much hidden from me?"

"You didn't *want* to know." Emma heaved a sigh. "Haven't you figured it out by now?"

"Well . . . yes," I admitted. "But I'd thought no one else would."

"Everybody will know it if you publish this, but so what?"

"I didn't understand that my grieving the loss of my mother would keep me from being a comfort to you. I'm sorry."

"Listen here. That wasn't it at all. You were the only one I kept it from for a reason: First off, I couldn't keep it from anyone else in my congregation; everyone knew everything about everybody! But you lived across the Ohio River, so when we talked on the phone I could actually feel like I really *was* healthy, that I would recover and we would have Margaritas . . . or Coconut Chews . . . or a dip in the pool, a trip to the mall, add to our bracelets . . . you know?"

I nodded. I was beginning to really understand. She feared she was dying but she wanted to *feel* like she wasn't. She could accomplish that as long as I didn't see her in person.

"Do you have any regrets?" I asked.

"Don't even get me started," Emma said.

"I guess it's not important now anyway."

Emma smiled. "When it's your time to go you'll meet me here, and then you'll remember we've been here before. We can't bring our past with us because the baggage would be too much, and totally useless I might add.

But you'll remember. Life never stops. We really do live forever, just not in Paradise on Earth. You and me? We've a whole lot more adventures ahead of us, girlfriend."

I sat for awhile, thinking of all the exciting possibilities ahead for Emma and me.

"Your mother was here, but she left the month after I arrived. She decided to go back in the form of your granddaughter, Greta. But you know that, don't you?"

"I've highly suspected it, yes."

"Greta was named after Gretchen, so how could your mom resist?"

That brought a smile to my face. "What about Jim? He died one year after you did."

"Oh, he's around here somewhere. I can't keep track of everybody."

A long pause ensued. I wondered if she'd gone away.

"I love what you've done to your living room. You always did like pink."

I laughed. "Thanks. I'm thinking about redoing it in all white."

"That'll be nice, too. White . . . so clean, pure and innocent. I like it."

"So . . . we're all good then?"

"We're good," Emma said. "Sure we are—always have been, you goofball! Now go on and finish this book and find joy with the rest of your life!"

CHAPTER FIFTY-SEVEN
THE FINAL CHAPTER

How does one write "The Final Chapter" of a memoir when there are many pages of one's life yet to be lived?

I've described my excitement as a child when I found The Truth, the questions and doubts that gradually filtered in and the hurdles I maneuvered as I backed away from religion's grasp. I've portrayed the joy of motherhood, the fun of grand-parenting and the unequaled satisfaction of having a best friend like Emma. I've been an "open book" in recounting my mistakes in judgment, although I prefer to call them *learning experiences*. I've laid myself wide open to the anger and despair I suffered with the deaths of those I loved and the despondency from being unwanted and tossed out of places where I thought I belonged.

It was not my intention to create a tribute to my mother, but as it turned out, it is her story, and mine. While I was not conscious of this previously, I now realize my continuation as a Jehovah's Witness was more about my relationship with my very real mother than with a perceived god. While The Truth was a shelter, a safety net, and kept me safe from harm, I may not have discovered it if it hadn't been for her—seeking answers to her young daughter's questions about God and life itself. Mom was my genuine cocoon, my hammock to swing in and hide out of sight from the rest of the world. Life is not an emergency, a fact my mother understood, and she showed me how to live it without urgency. I'm thankful to have shared a psychologically healthy mother/daughter relationship with Gretchen. It's worthy of note that while Mom waited until after *her* mother's death to find The Truth, I waited until after Mom's death to leave it, which probably runs parallel to the fact that after someone we love dies, we redefine ourselves.

During Mom's illness, we'd talked about how difficult it was for her that night at the meeting when I was disfellowshipped. She'd tried not to cry, but to no avail. Several people had offered words of sympathy, as though it was the end of the world, but one very dear sister suggested a more positive approach: "Gretchen, try not to worry. Wait and see—Joanna's final chapter hasn't been written yet."

"So, Mom, here it is: my final chapter. It's quite okay that you didn't "get" Star Wars, a science fiction movie with sequels and prequels that probably wouldn't have interested you either. But my book is not fiction, it's real—the story of your daughter's life. I'm still the same girl I always was; only my viewpoint has changed, but I'm pretty sure you saw that coming. I have no doubt you get me—you always did."

~*~

Who doesn't like a happy, grand finale? In the end there is praise for Craig. He stands quietly *aside,* allowing me to be my mercurial, up and down self; he stands *beside*, holding my hand to ground me when sudden mood swings make it difficult for me to keep both feet on the ground, on those days when I threaten to move to the moon.

I treated Craig to a Jimmy Buffet concert in downtown Louisville for his birthday. We sat in a booth at The Spaghetti Factory for dinner before the performance, and I caught him smiling at me.

"What? Do I have sauce on my face?"

He laughed. "I love you."

I had not expected that from him. Craig signs my birthday and anniversary cards with an "I love you" and he'll end a phone conversation with "love you" but he rarely, if ever, actually *says* those three words.

"You *still* love me? I don't see how you can after all I've put you through," I said. His glance roamed the room, searching for an appropriate response. We locked eyes and he said, "I'd have to say our really good times are so much more than good. They're *grand!*"

THE END

ABOUT THE AUTHOR

Joanna Foreman's short fiction has appeared in The Indian Creek Anthology Series; Melange-Books; and her own collection, *Ghostly Hauntings of Interstate-65*. She grew up in Indianapolis, Indiana, raised her family in Louisville, Kentucky and currently resides in Georgetown, Indiana. For more information, visit www.joannaforeman.com.

CPSIA information can be obtained at www.ICGtesting.com
Printed in the USA
LVOW01s1926180214

374220LV00022B/442/P

9 780615 934723